TUNING IN TO THE
GOD FREQUENCY

Tuning In to the
GOD FREQUENCY

The prayer that changes everything.

MICHAEL T. ABADIE

TUNING IN TO THE GOD FREQUENCY
THE PRAYER THAT CHANGES EVERYTHING.

iUniverse books may be ordered through booksellers or by contacting:

iUniverse LLC
1663 Liberty Drive
Bloomington, IN 47403
www.iuniverse.com
1-800-Authors (1-800-288-4677)

ISBN: 978-1-4917-4439-0 (sc)
ISBN: 978-1-4917-4440-6 (e)

Printed in the United States of America.

iUniverse rev. date: 08/14/2014

The Nelson Study Bible, New King James Version, copyright 1997

The Holy Bible King James Version, The Crusade Analytical Study Edition, Crusade Bible Publishers, Inc, copyright 1970

CONTENTS

Endless thanks to Ken Adams for the gracious provision of his photograph entitled "Sunrise Cloud Dance" that became the cover of this book.

Thank you, Elizabeth Badeaux for your creativity in graphic design and enthusiastic willingness to go the extra mile.

DEDICATION

This book is dedicated primarily to Christ Jesus, my Lord, and the angels in His command, who, during my "wild" years kept me alive long enough to finally be of some benefit to my fellow man. By the acceptance of His mercy and grace and by following the Holy footprints carefully set before me, illusive dreams of the past have become present realities.

I also dedicate this book to the love of my life, my wife Diane, who is the epitome of a dream blessed and brought into this present life.

DREAMS

Would it be that dreams
Were known to fly
On reality's glorious wings

Would it that they
At beckoned call
Would depart from Queens
and Kings

To visit those of earthly state
And magically bestow
The sun, the moon and all the stars
Simply that we could know

Dreams were created for all mankind
With faith to grant them flight
Ushering the wondrous unseen world
From hope, to faith, to sight

By Michael T. Abadie
June, 1998

IN THE BEGINNING

"Good night Momma, good night Daddy. I love you and I'll see you in the morning; sleep tight," and the lights went out…and the darkness covered my room. The house would become almost silent except for the crickets, the settling noises in the attic, and the whooshing of the sheets as I quickly pulled them over my whole little body to hide myself from whatever may lurk in the bedroom while I lay helpless under the covers. *Now I lay me down to sleep; I pray the Lord my soul to keep. If I should die before I wake…*—if I should what? Just what the heck is THAT supposed to mean?? Why am I praying "if I should die before I wake"? The whole reason for this prayer is to keep me alive and protect me from being hurt or scared to death or eaten by something horrible while I'm lying here. Dying is not what I'm praying about! *I pray the Lord my soul to take.* Oh my gosh! If my soul is taken by God, then the rest of me will go with it and the worst of my childhood nightmares will come to pass because the only people with God are DEAD PEOPLE! I have seen dead people at funerals and they look creepy. If I had to be with all those dead guys, I would probably have a heart attack and end up having to die again. "Daaaaddyyyyyyyy, I don't want to die and see dead people!!" My Mom would always ask, *Did you say your prayers, Mike?* "That's why I'm scared. I don't want to die before I wake."

Sometime later, although I can't remember exactly when, I was taught by my Baptist parents to pray differently, "like the grown-ups pray," with the hope that this new direction would ease my little mind. After methodically memorizing every word exactly as the "King James" version of the Bible stated, each night before going to sleep the "Lord's Prayer" from the sixth chapter of Matthew became my regular mantra. Surely it would protect me from anything between bedtime and the next night when I prayed again. The implication was that the prayer seemed to have a 24-hour shelf life after being recited, although I wasn't specifically told that. If I did temporarily forget to pray the prayer, sleep would be impossible until the special spiritual words were said. When the final words left my lips—*for thine is the Kingdom and the power and the glory forever, Amen*—almost magically peaceful sleep would descend upon me along with the surety of waking up unscathed, uneaten, and alive. Every morning as my eyes opened to the welcome sunshine, I once again found myself to be just fine, complete with all ten fingers and toes, and all my other parts intact. This was valid proof to a young mind that God was listening. My faith in the power of the prayer increased.

During my early years our family attended the local Baptist church every Sunday and Wednesday. My parents even directed the high school youth group for a time. Prayers were very much an integral part of our lives. Depending upon someone much bigger than ourselves brought comfort and helped us decode the parables of life that popped up from time to time. During those days, the idea that the all-powerful God Who created everything

Our Father
which art in Heaven, Hallowed be thy
name. Thy kingdom come. Thy will
be done in earth, as it is in Heaven.
Give us this day our daily bread.
And forgive us our debts, as we
forgive our debtors. And lead us not
into temptation, but deliver us from
evil: For thine is the kingdom, and
the power, and the glory, for ever.
Amen.

When they had twisted a crown of thorns, they put it on His head, and a reed in His right hand. And they bowed the knee before Him and mocked Him, saying, "Hail, King of the Jews!" Then they spat on Him, and took the reed and struck Him on the head. And when they had mocked Him, they took the robe off Him, put His own clothes on Him, and led Him away to be crucified. Matthew 27:29-31

actually cared for us and even knew our names was consoling. However, the concept that His Son, Jesus, had to die so that we could be saved and forgiven was terribly confusing and disturbing for a young kid.

At the time of the Easter weekend, amidst the new clothes and uncomfortable shoes, the passion play would drive the point home in an attempt to include as much of the gruesome details of the crucifixion that a church production could deliver. I never did like those passion plays and still don't. Knowing that it happened once is more than enough to think about. Why was it that God's only son had to die such a dreadful death when the prayer I was taught to pray came from Him? How in the world could it protect me if it didn't protect Him from all the horrible stuff that was written about in the Bible and shown in those Easter plays?

During the rest of the year the weekly sermons, all thrown together into the mind of a child, tended to become really messed up. And the spiritual comfort, so desperately needed, just did not seem to make it out from under all the hell, fire, and brimstone messages blasted from the pulpit. I can remember our preacher shaking his finger in the air and professing at the top of his lungs that some people will burn in hell and on an appointed day some will be taken while others would be left behind. And those who remained here would experience a horrible end in a world, wracked by pain and suffering as fire rained down from the sky. Some of the church people would cry; sometimes the preacher would cry too and a few people would walk slowly down to the front while we sang a song. Then it would all be over until next time and the people would smile again. Strangely, the church adults seemed to understand it all and appeared to know why it was supposed to happen that way. At the end of each sermon, as we all walked to the door and shook the preacher's hand, the grown-ups would always congratulate him on what a great message it was. The preacher seemed to be an okay guy when he shook my hand, but to a little kid the message had been anything but great. It was a terrible thing to think about but every night in my bed, I would faithfully repeat the Lord's Prayer and pray that I wouldn't have to see all that stuff the preacher talked about. I prayed that if my dad and mom were taken on that special day that I would be good enough to go along with them so I wouldn't have to live with somebody else during the terrible coming times. Faith at the time was a regularly used word, but fear was the actual operative gorilla in the room. As I think back on those sermons, it seems that fear is mostly what I remember, and faith, if it was there, must have been hiding in the shadows.

Could You, Would You, Can You?

With adults as well as children, fear is often the greatest motivator of earnest and genuinely heartfelt but sometimes misguided prayer. During my lifetime, I know

> "Ask and it will be given to you; seek and you will find"
>
> Matthew 7:7

that I have been guilty of innumerable misguided prayers. Consequently, on that subject I do speak from experience. Today many people only pray as a means of rescue during bouts of trouble or in times of a perceived need or want rather than as the avenue of ongoing fellowship it is meant to be. God (or Jesus or the Holy Spirit) is sometimes treated as a great spiritual Santa Claus who can give us what we want or take away what we don't want. The television preacher says "Jeeeezzusss" will give us all we ask for because the Bible says so. All that the listeners have to do is repeat the right words with their hand on the TV for the desired results and send the check (as an obligatory demonstration of *faith)* to the address on the TV screen. When the latest anointed trinket arrives in the mailbox, *POOF,* everything should be just fine. You just can't help but wonder what Jesus would have to say about that.

It seems that the whole idea of prayer for many people has taken a wrong turn somewhere between Jerusalem and here, and has had a hard time getting through the cactus patch of misconception, deception, and misdirection. In some instances the practice of prayer has become a repetition of various forms of "could you; would you; can you; please provide; please forgive; give me, give me, give me. And dear Lord, if you do, I won't eat chocolate for a month and when the Lenten season is here, I'll try to keep from cursing." Although mildly dramatized, I have actually heard this type of horse trading theology in action, giving credibility to the assumption that God **must** have a great sense of humor to still love us even in our absolute goofiness. If He didn't find it humorous, some of us would be a crispy offering at the sacrificial altar of stupidity by now.

Realistically, the only successful way to have any kind of a relationship with anyone is to talk to them with honesty and respect on an ongoing basis. A relationship with the Lord is much the same. What if every morning I greeted my wife with, "Thank you for all you've done and today I ask that you bless ME and provide for ME and that you help everything to go MY way and you know I love you." And during the rest of the day you say nothing else except to note at bedtime, "Today you were great. Thanks for all those things you did for ME and I ask that you let ME sleep comfortably and peacefully. Please overlook anything I may have done to offend you." And you doze off to sleep. The next day and each day and night thereafter, you utter the same phrases and repeat the same words, never pausing to hear what your wife may have to say, never respectfully listening for a reply or input from her. With that analogy, it is easy to see that a relationship of that type is only one-sided and in fact is not a true relationship after all but merely a repetitive series of self-serving requests and statements. If that is the only ongoing dialog then there is no relationship existing between you, but rather a feeble attempt to fill the would-be silence with weightless words of no real or lasting value. The prayers of countless well-meaning Christians are similar to this scenario because they just have not been taught to pray thoughtfully.

When verbally relating to God, the practice referred to as prayer is a holy conversation to be carried out with ultimate respect. It was originally taught to believers for the purpose of uniting our spirit and the Holy Spirit in an embrace of comfort and trust in unity with our loving God. The fact is that Jesus outlined a basic blueprint of what and how to pray, with instructions concerning personal intent and spiritual awareness to be understood before the prayer begins. Not much reading is needed in the sixth chapter of Matthew before His words begin to shine through the fog of general misunderstanding to illuminate the original intent and purpose of the prayer known to most as the "Lord's Prayer," the "Our Father," or simply the prayer of Jesus in Matthew 6.

Just like millions of other believers, I prayed the Lord's Prayer consistently, word for word, straight out of the original King James edition for decades. While not fully understanding the scope of many of the phrases, I assumed that I would be blessed anyway because of the faithful and accurate repetition of the prayer. It is a curious thing how so many of us have mundanely retraced the cow path of unquestioning obedience by following the multitudes before us over the smooth and straight trail of ritual. Many never question why we do things the way we do. Some philosophies note that God may be offended and punish us if we dare to insult Him by questioning His methods. All the while we are reminded by some of those same teachers how we serve a loving and merciful God who forgives freely and loves us unconditionally, even when we mess up things. Maybe it's just me, but those schools of thought are diametrically opposed to common logic. God cares so much for each of us that He gave His only Son to die that terrible death as payment in full for all of our sins, so why would the same God punish His loving children for asking questions concerning areas that we don't understand? Even marginally intelligent people realize that questions based in honesty are imperative for learning what we don't know. And God being all-knowing must realize the precept of the believer's need to broaden spiritual awareness and comprehension in order to foster a firmer foundation for our spiritual cohesion. In fact the scriptures do not cover every facet of everything, and while detailing certain instances, are vague in other areas. For instance, the Bible doesn't have anything to say about me sitting here writing this book and about you reading it. But here we are (it looks real to me!). Is it written in the scriptures? NO. Is it a present reality? Yes. It seems that portions of the scriptures may be more of an outline for us to have on a "need to know" basis in order to teach and help during our visitation of earthly life. The fact is our Creator loves and understands us even more than our earthly parents could and will. At an appointed time only known to Him, He will transport our spirits into the glorious realm known as Heaven, governed by and presided over by our eternal God. According to the Bible and writings of most other major spiritual teachings, we are to eventually come into the Kingdom of the Most High God and abide continually in the true essence of the holiest form of unconditional eternal love that exists.

The concept from our earthly perception may be hard to visualize simply because we have nothing here to compare it with. Many years ago, I played music in a band and our keyboard player was blind from birth. He was a fabulous, gifted keyboard player, drummer, and singer, and the blindness was never a hindering factor in his performances. We were on a fifteen-minute break during a particular "gig" and Vann and I were sitting outside talking when he made an unusual request. "Explain to me what you see. Tell me all about where we are and what it looks like to you." I began by telling him that the day was perfect and clear, and the grass in back of the club where we were playing was a beautiful shade of green. Vann asked "What does *green* look like?" I paused while discovering I had no words to help him understand the concept of green because he had never seen or experienced it. He could feel the blades of grass, smell its fragrance, and touch the place where the parking lot ended and the grass started, but its color could only be imagined by him because he had nothing to compare it with. Of the hundreds of music jobs I've played and the countless conversations I've had with other musicians, that special fifteen-minute break was unforgettable.

When discussing the reality of an eternal afterlife, some would reply "show me and I will believe." In other words, prove it! However, Bible teachings note that the things seen through earthly eyes, the tangibles, are only temporary and will in time be no more. On the other hand, the things we can't presently see are actually the only things of eternally lasting significance. Consider the writings of Paul, "…while we do not look at the things which are seen, but at the things which are not seen. For the things which are seen are temporary, but the things which are not seen are eternal" (2 Corinthians 4:18). In this present time of rampant material worship where ownership and the checkbook balance reign supreme, it is easy to see the 180 degree paradox that thrives in the world of illusionary tangibility. I've seen the bumper sticker that states "Whoever dies with the most toys wins!" While moderately funny, it is also sad to think that some people actually seem to believe in the idea. These deceived souls should be taken on a short excursion to the nearest funeral home in order to view the cruel reality that hearses are not equipped with trailer hitches for a reason. To live an entire lifetime believing that we are coincidentally born into this life to eventually die for no other reason except to fill some space for a time and impress our neighbors is a terribly sad and hollow philosophy. The "show me and I will believe" group should take a long, honest look in the nearest mirror to see if they actually believe all of the cells in a perfectly working and magnificently designed body machine just happened to fall into place as they did with no intelligent design or forethought. Consistent with that type of possibility thinking, the contents of several parts warehouses thrown together into a heap should have the potential to produce a Rolls Royce without the hand of an engineer or a mechanic.

WHATETH DOST THOU WANTEST?

Throughout the ages, humanity has grappled with the question of how to properly communicate with an eternally existing, all-knowing God. Historically the faithful have offered up everything from gifts of the finest crops, to animal and even human sacrifices in order to appease and convince the great Creator to keep the crops growing, the water flowing, continue the blessings, and provide everlasting life and a blissful existence. All over the world, from the dawn of recorded time, practiced techniques have ranged from ultimate simplicity to outrageously complex rituals. Even today controversy rages on, wedging its way between the various religions with each one believing it has found the "true way" into God's own heart. Unfortunately and tragically it is not uncommon to hear of those who scream "God is great" before pushing the detonator button to take lives and futures of innocent adults and children in order to please their "god." From the seemingly most holy and pious of ceremonies to the complete nonsense of ruthless and indiscriminate murdering and maiming, opinions differ wildly around the planet and even in our own neighborhoods concerning exactly what should be done or accomplished in order to persuade God to shower favor upon His believers.

What exactly are we to pray and how much should we pray in order to come into God's presence or at least ring His doorbell? Does dropping to our knees or lying prostrate exhibit submission and show that we are woefully humble before Him? Should we raise our hands or bow our heads? If we deprive ourselves of food or even life-giving water and pray ceremoniously while doing so, is He more likely to hear our prayers? What should be done or said and how often are we to do or say it in order to be relatively certain that our earthly lamentations and supplications have the potential to reach the ears and heart of the most Supreme God?

> Learning to speak to God without attempting to sound like a voice track from a Robin Hood movie should be honestly refreshing and quite relaxing.

With a strange but familiar twist, many dinner blessings and Sunday morning services begin and end verbally with various "thee, thou, and thine" expressions and an occasional "wouldest" and "couldest" thrown in for good measure, all sounding wonderfully holy to the listeners. Although the prayers may be meant with all good intentions, the 16th century Old English inferences are not necessary. In 1611, when King James ordered printing of Bibles for the people, they were produced in the language that was current and common at the time and in the region. It is probably right to assume that God is not overly impressed by our often improper insertions of the kings

English into our prayers. The King James Version of the Bible is still the most favored translation and is reflected in our scripture quotations and resultant bleed-over into some of the prayer dialect we hear today. Realistically though, it's hard to imagine Jesus saying to the disciples "come thou hence" when His native language was first century Aramaic.

The point here and to be found throughout this book, is to find our prayer time in an honest and heartfelt spiritual atmosphere and to enjoy communion with our God who knows us better than we know ourselves. It is probably safe to surmise that He will not be impressed by our pretentious interpretation of spiritual vocabulary or by clever phrasing learned from the latest book on successful sales techniques. We don't have to sell and He doesn't need to buy. Learning to speak to God without attempting to sound like a voice track from a Robin Hood movie should be honestly refreshing and quite relaxing. Removing much of the underlying pressure to "sound holy" while praying helps the believer to focus on what is being conveyed as opposed to how it might or should sound. After all, our Lord knows our heart better than we do, making it a safe assumption that He is well aware of the true intentions of our communications.

So many messages are preached today that address what God expects of us when all the time the answer is right there, written down in black and white for all to see. Scripture, in 2 Chronicles 7:14, states, "If my people who are called by My name shall **humble** themselves, and pray and seek My face…" Humility and communication is the answer to volumes of sermons that ask the question, *what does God need from us or want from us and how do we please Him?* Humility as defined by *Strong's Exhaustive Concordance* *of the Bible* is "to bend the knee, to bring down (low), to humble (self)." Further examination of the definition of the word used in the Old Testament 2 Chronicles writing notes the phrase "into subjection." Evidently the act of and intention to (simply) be humble is how we should approach the spirit and presence of God according to the Bible. "Whosoever shall humble himself as this little child, the same is greatest in the kingdom of heaven" (Matthew 18:4) is the answer Jesus gave to the disciples when they expressed concern over who would be the greatest in the kingdom of Heaven. His comparison to the little child implies the idea of simply being "yourself." To humbly come before our Father as that little child who bows his knee—not to impress, but from humble subjection—is to appear in His presence as a faithful servant seeking only His will to be done in the life He has chosen to bless us with.

Simplistic honesty is not only implied but is also imperative for proper protocol in prayer to develop a meaningful holy relationship. Personal transparency is another facet of simplicity that increases along the same lines with spiritual awareness. Faith allows us to simply be who each of us was created to be, especially when praying to our Father God. In this present world of well-rehearsed charades and camouflaged ulterior motivations, transparency is a rare jewel of truth and courage confirmed in the lives of those not afraid to live in its freedom.

While examining the prayers of Jesus, the earnest and humble simplicity of His communication with the Father exemplifies the way prayer should be properly addressed. Generally speaking, if simplicity and humility were good enough for Jesus, they should be just fine for us.

Revelation of Supplication Motivation

The third chapter of the book of Ecclesiastes states, "To everything there is a season and a time to every purpose under Heaven." A portion of that chapter of the Old Testament actually became an international hit pop song named Turn, Turn, Turn, which was recorded by The Byrds in the mid-sixties with a generation of long-haired, bead-wearing bands and fans playing and unknowingly singing verses straight from the Bible's Old Testament.

After a personally solid, sobering, and life-altering salvation experience in the mid-seventies, my "season" of prayer once again returned to the merciful Lord who had saved me from my own devices and near destruction during those "out of control" years. Just as Solomon had written, the "time for every purpose" had knocked upon my door and caused my knees to bow to the truth of eternal reality. My salvation was unquestionable, but as all Christians know, receiving Christ does not mean that life's problems cease to arise. Several years later, Solomon's "time to laugh" had begun to fade and the "time to weep" became an all-too-frequent, unwelcome but familiar visitor.

To everything there is a season,
A time for every purpose under heaven;
A time to be born,
And a time to die:
A time to plant,
And a time to pluck what is planted:
A time to kill,
And a time to heal:
A time to break down,
And a time to build up:
A time to weep,
And a time to laugh:
A time to mourn,
And a time to dance:
A time to cast away stones,
And a time to gather stones:
A time to embrace,
And a time to refrain from embracing:
A time to gain,
And a time to lose:
A time to keep,
A time to throw away:
A time to tear,
And a time to sew:
A time to keep silence,
And a time to speak:
A time to love,
And a time to hate:
A time of war,
And a time of peace.
Ecclesiastes 3;1-8

The writings in Ecclesiastes are largely
attributed to King Solomon, son of King David,
both of whom are found in the lineage of Jesus.
The ecclesiastical principles are considered to be
wisdom from the ages with Solomon regularly
touted as one of the wisest men in the world,
even though at times he displayed very common
earthly shortcomings as humans tend to do.
Nevertheless, the words in that third chapter are
pure wisdom and accurately reflect times of
rejoicing and times of mourning and healing, times
of breaking down and building up again, all
proving that some things of this world have not
changed very much from the times of Solomon's
writings thought to be penned around 977 B.C.
All of us can testify to having our own
experiences of those seasons of ups and downs
noted by Solomon.

During a projected and emotionally painful time of personal distress, the words and principles of Ecclesiastes became personified in my life. It was during those tough times that the "Lord's Prayer" once again emerged as an old friend peeping out from the pages of the book of Matthew. The late evenings during that phase of my life consisted of a four and a half mile prayer walk beginning around 10:30 PM every night without fail. They were planned while the kids were in bed and the darkness served as a cover for the occasionally tearful walks through the streets of a nearby neighborhood. On one particular night during those trying years, the thought crossed my mind that the Lord might be tired of hearing my "please help me" woeful prayers and that a change of positive venue could be a breath of fresh air for both of us. In very short order, the formerly well rehearsed words "Our Father who art in Heaven" came from my lips in the traditional King James dialect, but this time with a deepening epiphany of what the prayer was originally designed to be. It seems that *someone* who loved and cared really wanted me to consider what those ancient words were meant to convey during the offering of the prayer. Unlike the prayers of my childhood, without motivation of doubt or fear, I began to thoughtfully recite the prayer learned so many years ago. As a child and even a young man, the prayer was usually droned in monotone with word after memorized word mindlessly quoted in quick order to get through it and say "amen," the end. But on this night, after the initial opening of the prayer came from my lips, a pause occurred as a new revelation began to unfold and the age-old supplication began to make sense to me, verse by verse. When Jesus taught the disciples how to pray during the Sermon on the Mount (Matthew 5:3-7:27), He chose every word and phrase in an express design with no spin and no flowery run-on phrases, just divine truth aligned in perfect order. Those words, ordained by God the Father, were given in the specific way and order in which they appear for a definite purpose.

On that exceptional night and the nights following, all those years ago, I learned an invaluable lesson in quieting my impatient soul to become "still" before my Father in order to listen to what was being stated in the "Lord's Prayer." The Messiah taught His disciples to "pray in this manner," and I thought what I had previously done was the same, but the enlightenment and understanding is what I had been lacking during countless times of hollow repetition. Cathedrals, churches, and chapels all produce a certain energy or feeling when entering the vestibule, but on that starlit night, the open doors of my inner temple produced an awareness of illumination incomparable to any previous earthly contentment.

Humble, simplistic reverence before God is the way it was always meant to be and the way it has been for thousands of years, until recent generations. During a relatively short span of time, the lights of our present "progress" and incessant *busy-ness* have taken center stage in the daily scramble experienced by all who live in its grip and are entangled in its chains. Humanity's understanding of quiet stillness has become but a dim recollection before our unchanging God. Mental and physical stillness in today's world have come to be forgotten companions to true depth in spiritual communication. How many people today legitimately long to hear the voice of God speak from that inner temple but can't find quiet time for long enough to hear the much needed message?

A worship song entitled "Be Still," has been sung in thousands of churches for many years. The lyrics are straight from the book of Psalms, chapter 46, verse 10. Those eight powerful words are all of the lyrics. The melody is simple but beautiful, quite easy to learn and sing, and tends to lead congregations into a quietly reverent time of spiritual introspection. Many times I have witnessed the quiet comfort of the "be still" message as it works its way to open the inner temple of those who truly seek its peace. While singing the song it is easy to overlook the commanding intent of the scripture, but God admonishes the reader to first "Be still" as the primary idea for what is to occur, which is to "know" that He is God. The original Hebrew word used for "still" is translated as "to abate, cease," meaning in short, everything else must stop— everything. The Hebrew word used for "know" means to certify or make known. In that short sentence we are told that in order to know, to certify, or to make known our connection and fellowship with God, the abating or ceasing necessary for stillness must without compromise first be in place. During my walk and prayer on that night of personal epiphany, I obeyed the "be still and know that I am God" scripture between phrases of the Lord's Prayer, and it changed me and the way I pray forever.

> "Be still
> and know
> that I am God."

Over the years I have led hundreds of worship services and taught many classes for differing congregations and denominations where the message of that song and the scripture from which it came made life-changing differences for people. The importance of learning stillness is rarely preached and consequently not widely practiced in most disciplines. The concept must first be learned before it can be effectively taught. And that takes time—precious time. Stillness isn't generally attributed to the everyday layman but rather to those spiritually advanced personalities such as priests, nuns, monks, or shamans cloistered away from the world practicing vows of silence. Psalms 46:10 makes the point that all people who truly seek to know the presence of God must first be still. Loosely translated into today's vernacular; turn off the noise, get away from the confusion, and even be brave enough to turn off the blasted cell phone for a while. It may be a tough blow to the cherished egos of those who have no other use for their non-dominant hand, but the earth will continue to turn and the social and business worlds will go on as usual while a cell phone is silenced for a time.

With today's ongoing technology barrage vying for every moment of the public's attention, quiet time for the multitudes has come to be an unknown and seldom if ever practiced diversion. From the computer screen at work to personal sound systems blasting during drive or ride time to the television, computer, and phone screens where we live, the idea of respectful silence for spiritual contemplation has become lost in a non-stop menagerie of multi-tasking and informational infusions. With the previously stated understanding that true worship demands quiet time before God, it is easy to put the pieces of the busy puzzle together to see the fork in the road. Would the shepherds on the hills of Bethlehem have seen the star if they would have been glued to an I-Phone screen texting friends? Would the Magi have witnessed the greatest birth in the history of the world because the music in their ear buds was too loud? While sounding a bit nonsensical, the point is that distractions today are so numerous and overwhelming that we have come to not recognize them as such. It only takes a moment to look around and observe what the general population has become. A recent news cast highlighted an "app" for cell phones that allows the texting person to see ahead of them in order to prevent some of the numerous *fall injuries* occurring as a result of people watching the screen instead of watching where they are walking. In some cases the craziness is welcomed because the busy life is seen in social and most business circles as a mark of success and affluence. With the best of intentions in mind, even our sanctuaries have become virtual ant beds of non-stop activities, rehearsals, and nightly committee meetings where the *busy-ness* can easily become confused with spiritual productivity, and quiet time before our Lord becomes a rarity even in the leadership. The fact today stands out more than ever that if you find yourself too busy (even with things at the church) to read from God's word regularly and to spend quality time in prayer and reflection with our Lord, then you have become unbalanced and lacking in the most fundamental element of spirituality.

Rather than seeking non-stop movement or entertainment from a constant inflow of auditory and visual input characteristically producing little redeeming value, regular visits to the quiet and calm of the temple within will be found as a welcome relief from the attention-stealing melodrama. Peace and negatively-charged drama are energies that cannot co-exist with the presence of one indicating the absence of the other. Usually, negative emotions are born in fear and doubt where, on the other end of the scale, peace is a product of positive faith. When active faith is present, fear and doubt are nowhere to be found. Conversely, a person who lives under the oppressive weight of fear may have a hard time understanding the concept of faith. And that brings us back around to the importance of stillness and the peaceful openness found within its specter. Sometimes, the most effective prayer of peace is found in the faithful silence of stillness before God.

Scripture found in 1 Corinthians 6:19 informs us that our body is the temple of the Holy Ghost, implying that if we are in search of the Holy Spirit or Holy Ghost, it can be found dwelling within the body of the believer. That's right—**inside**! Here's a thought: If you are in the habit of asking the Holy Spirit to please be with you, quit asking and begin thanking Him for His indwelling presence as confirmed in the Bible. Ironically, I have personally heard numerous pastors and parishioners pray "Lord, we ask you to please be with us today." If there is a question concerning the whereabouts of His presence, then someone is not reading the Bible, which I also refer to as "the manufacturer's handbook." Furthermore, where is faith found in that prayer? If the congregation and the pastor are Christian believers, the glorified Spirit of Christ came in the door with every one of them as scripture states! Asking for His presence is not necessary and exhibits a lack of faith and understanding. Thanking Him for His love and expressing gratitude for abiding with us is the way we should pray. If faith to believe is the problem, scripture also has an answer for that in Romans 10:17, "So then faith comes by hearing, and hearing by the word of God." And of course, the word of God is found in the Bible. A short study of Jesus' teachings concerning the indwelling by the Holy Spirit in the book of John will prove the point without question.

Actually, according to scripture in Acts, our churches are not the temple of God or the house of God as is loosely proclaimed from countless pulpits. I can only imagine the collective gasps from those readers who can't believe this statement. But before tossing this book into the fireplace and making plans to burn me at the stake, take a look at Acts 17:24 that plainly states, "God, who made the world and everything in it, since He is Lord of Heaven and earth, **does not dwell in temples made with hands**." The truth of that scripture can be life-changing for those who just didn't know. It changed *my* life. With the advent of the Holy Spirit (the resurrected form of Christ), the believers became His temple. As members of the body of Christ are united in faith, the church is present whether in a building or not. I've gone to "church" on the side of the road sitting on a motorcycle. Yes, among other things I am a biker and have had glorious coast to coast prayer meetings from the seat of my motorcycles because the

Holy Spirit is not afraid to ride. Rain doesn't rattle Him and lightning doesn't scare Him. His Spirit is not limited to certain areas or to motorcycles or cars or to a tree with markings that resemble the face of Jesus or Mary. I have enjoyed His presence in the woods, on the beach, in many cities, and generally everywhere I've been because the Holy Spirit truly does live within me as He does in every other believer whether we *feel* it or not. His presence is not based upon our feelings, thank God.

Shortly after Jesus' resurrection, the prophecy in John 14:20 became fulfilled: "At that day you shall know that I am in my Father and you in me, **and I in you.**" Jesus promised to abide with us. Abide does not mean to "visit occasionally only if you're good." Rather it translates "stay" or "reside" as evidenced by the scripture in Hebrews 13:5, "For He has said, I will never leave you or forsake you." Note the word "never." The Spirit of Jesus the Christ, our Messiah, lives or abides within the body temple of the believer and as stated will never leave or forsake us. That truth is an invaluable asset

> God's presence is not contained by walls and certainly not within walls designed by committees and built by human hands.

during the times when we allow fear to override our faith and it seems to us that our prayers bounce off the ceiling as if they are of no avail. No matter how we may feel, the Holy Spirit remains present. No matter what we may think, the temple within is open all twenty four hours of everyday without fail. We must remember that feelings are pure emotion and emotions change regularly, as do our thoughts. Circumstances change. Even the earth is in a constant state of change; our friends and acquaintances change, and whether or not we like to admit it, we change along with our concepts and interpretations of right and wrong. Our Lord, however, is eternal and is the "same yesterday, today and forever" (Hebrews 13:8). In other words, He changes not. His truth in years past is still truth today. What a solid anchor He is in the restless sea of an unstable world.

THE NEED FOR HEED

The sixth chapter of Matthew opens with a cautionary note from Jesus, stating, "Take heed" in the first two words of verse one with the Sermon on the Mount already in progress. "Take heed that you do not your charitable deeds (or alms in some translations) before men, to be seen by them. Otherwise you have no reward from your Father in Heaven." In His teaching of radically new standards, the practices and hypocritical motivations of the Pharisees are chastised and basically used as examples of what not to do. Jesus does not mince words as He testifies to and warns against what He has witnessed from the religious elite of the day in the synagogues and on the streets of Jerusalem. The listeners, including His disciples, are sternly admonished against following the examples of the Scribes and Pharisees' self-serving motivations in order to appear outwardly pious before the eyes and ears of the bystanders.

Referring to the practice of alms giving or charitable giving to the poor and under-privileged, Jesus notes that giving should be done in secrecy without public display, not with sounding trumpets as the Pharisees do. It is recorded that before alms giving, a literal trumpet was sounded under the pretense of alerting the poor, but also called attention to those who were giving, much like some of today's politicians and those in the public's eye at various photo opportunities and televised press conferences. "Therefore, when you do a charitable deed, do not sound a trumpet before you as the hypocrites do in the synagogues and in the streets that they may have glory from men. Assuredly, I say to you, they have their reward." The gift and the blessing should be known to only the giver and receiver so that the Father will also see in secret and will reward the giver openly. "But when you do a charitable deed, do not let your left hand know what your right hand is doing, that your charitable deed may be in secret; and your Father who sees in secret will Himself, reward you openly." Addressing the act of prayer in verse 5, Jesus warns again to not be like the hypocrites because they love to pray standing in prominent places, in order to be seen by all. "And when you pray, you shall not be like the hypocrites. For they love to pray standing in the synagogues and on the corners of the streets, that they may be seen by men. Assuredly, I say to you they have their reward." There are evidently no heavenly rewards to be given for that

> "Therefore, when you do a charitable deed, do not sound a trumpet before you as the hypocrites do in the synagogues and in the streets that they may have glory from men. Assuredly, I say to you, they have their reward."

kind of religiously blatant showmanship at that time or at any other time. Rather, in verse 6, "when you pray, go into your room and when you have shut your door, pray to your Father who is in the secret place; and your Father who sees in secret will reward you openly." During this discourse, Jesus leaves nothing to the imagination in explaining the sanctity of prayer as opposed to the side-show techniques He has witnessed. He has no problem with calling hypocrisy by name and pointing out the most blatant offenders in the process.

Verse seven drops an ideological bombshell on common practices of that time still quite common today. "But when you pray, **do not use vain repetitions** as the heathen do: for they think that they will be heard for their many words." In this scripture "vain repetitions" is defined as "meaningless words." The point is made quite clear in the words "do not." An interesting observation found here is the fact that Jesus preached very few negative messages containing the "do not" clause. The vast majority of His teachings were in a positive vein, further characterizing the positive nature and energy of the Messiah. It is thought-provoking to notice that the firmly stated "do not" messages noted here are related to the practices of those thought of as the religious hierarchy of the day and as a warning to the general populace to not follow their egotistical examples. Jesus implied the quantity of words is not what makes the difference but the quality and sincerity of the words are essential for a properly respectful prayer. In a supportive scripture, Matthew 12:34 states: "…for out of the abundance of the heart the mouth speaks," further clarifying the importance of "a clean heart." The subject was also spoken of generations earlier by King David in Psalms 51:10 as he prayed for restoration and forgiveness: "Create in me a clean heart, O God: and renew a right spirit within me." From the original Hebrew, the word "heart" is widely used concerning the feelings, will, and even intellect. Conversation with our Father should follow the honestly simplistic, straight from the heart standard of the "little child" entering the throne room with love and respect.

Matthew 6:8 contains yet another "not," as Jesus once again cautions the listeners to "not" be like the temple hypocrites and adds a very interesting side light: "For your Father knows the things you have need of before you ask Him." The key words to contemplate in this part of the verse are "knows" and "need."

How many prayers have been prayed begging God for something believed to be an urgent and imminent need only to discover later that we were actually glad the prayer was not answered according to our request? If honest enough to admit it, we have all had the experience at one time or another. The mortal mind of even the most sincere believer cannot know for sure what may be found around the next curve in the road and it's often revealed that today's desires can become tomorrow's regrets. Life teaches new truths daily if we are open to learning the lessons. The fact is, we think we know what we "need" by the dictates of the ever-present ego, but our thoughts and God's wisdom are light years apart. We think; He knows. Bearing in mind that faith is the chief operational component of Christianity, the person who comes before God should already have in place the trust and faith, not only to believe but also to know that God supplies what we need, when we need it. Not according to our whims and emotionally driven plans, and certainly not dependent upon what other people think, God provides by His perfect will.

In the following five verses of Matthew chapter 6, a ground-shaking new model or concept of prayer is revealed, contrary to the ritualistic and impersonal temple recitations commonly practiced at the time. By following this prayer directive, the everyday person is granted the privilege to speak directly to the Father in a personal dialog including permission to ask for redemption from sins, removing the need for a high priest middleman to do the bidding. Bear in mind that Jesus is a Jew and at this point in His life His ministry was targeting the Jews with His arrival as the "King of the Jews." Writings of the apostle Paul recorded in Romans 1:16 verify the gospel was primarily intended for the Jews, "for the Jew **first** and also for the Greek" (also referred to as Gentiles). Having previously noted scriptures cautioning the people not to be as the Pharisees and Scribes obviously denotes Judaism. As such, Jesus instructs them in a new and revolutionary concept and model of prayer, "In this manner, therefore, pray." "In this manner" does not necessarily mean to use only these words and phrases—remembering that Jesus spoke against meaningless, empty repetition—but rather to frame the prayer in a properly reverent and appropriate structure in order to address the Most High God.

THE GRAND OPENING

It is almost common knowledge that the prayer taught by Jesus begins with "Our Father, who is in Heaven," but those six opening, all-important words set the divine tone for the entire prayer. This greeting builds the foundation for who is being addressed, what His relationship is to His followers, and declares that His residence is not of this earth. Jesus prayed **OUR** Father, attesting that we corporately share the same heavenly spiritual Father.

> *"Our Father who is in heaven"*

Throughout the Bible, name designations for God are prevalent, such as El, El Shaddai, Immanuel, Elohim, Yahweh, Yahweh-tsidkenu, Jehovah, Adonai, and more, with the names defining particular attributes of his deity. Old Testament writings indicate the Israelites became afraid when the awesome manifestation of God was present. Due to God's unfathomable power, the people could not relate to Him and hid or ran away for fear of being in His presence. During that early period, it was Moses who was chosen as God's mouthpiece to relate to the people. But during a later time, at the advent of the man Jesus as the Son of God, everyday people could view someone who was also born from a woman and looked like people of that region, someone they could relate to and believe in when he spoke of the availability of mercy, grace, and forgiveness of sins. It was Jesus who became the human incarnation of holiness who could personally assure the people their sins were forgiven. The populace could easily relate to Him from a more personal and intimate standpoint; and He referred to God as Father.

In the prayer, designation of the name "Father" is translated as "parent," implicating the Father God, Creator of all, as a heavenly spiritual parent who freely provides access for His children to approach Him. The word "who" further solidifies His personal connection with humanity, followed by the name of His residence as an obviously different realm or dimension in a place referred to as "Heaven."

> Think of heaven and your mind imagines God. Think of God and the idea of heaven is already there.

How many times has the term *Heavenly Father* been used as a way to describe God without another thought concerning where He resides and what this heavenly place is all about? The subject of Heaven is not usually taught in our churches because the writings describing it are vague to say the least. In a general sense, God and Heaven are always linked together, as one being an inseparable part of the other. Heaven has been and still is a subject of many an abstract speculative discussion. Think of heaven and your mind imagines God. Think of God and the idea of heaven is already there. Separation of the two entities is difficult from a conceptual point of view. Although partially described by some people who have been involved in near-death experiences, perception of a timeless presence in an eternally wonderful and completely spiritual place is one born only in the imagination and hope of those of us who have yet to visit heaven. Biblical writings indicate that Jesus descended from heaven, and after His resurrection was "taken up" to heaven in full view of eye witnesses. First Thessalonians 4:16-17 states the Lord will descend from heaven at the end of this age to retrieve the righteous resurrected dead along with believers who are alive during the time. In a message of comfort to His disciples, Jesus referred to heaven as His Father's house where He was going to prepare a place for believers. King David, the psalmist, referred to his place of eternal residence as "the house of the Lord" at the end of the 23rd Psalm, and noted, "And I will dwell in the house of the Lord Forever." In Jesus' painful conversation with the criminal on the cross of crucifixion next to Him, Paradise was the descriptive name used for the place of blessed happiness. If there is an exact geographical location of "heaven" it remains unknown to those of us who have not yet witnessed it, but the fact that Jesus spoke of it gives it unquestioned credibility and a reality much greater than what our limited senses can provide in the earthly realm.

One such memorable and thought-provoking discussion about heaven occurred many years ago when my youngest son Brett, then only four and a half years old, was playing on the kitchen floor while I made a pot of afternoon coffee. Never looking up from his favorite toy truck on the floor, he asked, "Dad, does God live in heaven?" Quite an insightful question to be asked by such a little guy, I thought, so I answered quickly, "Yes He does, according to the Bible." After a short time, the second question came forth, "Dad, where is heaven?" And there was the proverbial age-old question zinged at me from a four and a half-year-old kid with a toy truck in his hand! Without much hesitation, I attempted to describe the possibilities in a manner from which Brett might glean at least a small piece of spiritual insight. The explanation shouldn't mention "realms" or "planes of existence" or "dimensions" because he would be more confused than informed by the end of the discussion. So, in the most simplistic manner I said "some people believe it is way up there (pointing up). Some people believe it is all around us but we just can't see it (parallel plane). And some people think it may even be inside of us (the kingdom within), but nobody really knows for sure." As my simplified theoretic explanation ended, Brett put his truck back down on the floor and began to push it around, making "truck noises." Only a few seconds passed and the third question came forth. "Does God ever talk to people? "Yes He does," I answered confidently. Brett immediately asked

> "Then why doesn't He tell anybody where He lives?"

"Then why doesn't He tell anybody where He lives?" A moment of silence was required, followed by an elongated pause to retrieve my jaw from the kitchen floor. And another moment of wondering why anyone I know, including clergy, had never thought to ask that question or put together that chain of reasoning. I had always preached the attributes of truthfulness to my kids as the only way to live and all I could do now was what I taught them to do. I looked at Brett's inquisitive little brown eyes and humbly confessed, "I really never thought of it that way and I just don't really know. I'm sorry, but if I ever get a chance to find out, I will. And I've got to tell you that is one heck of a question, especially from a guy your age." After a time of utter wonder and personal silent reflection, the world around me began to turn again on its axis as before. The coffee pot made a gurgling sound and the sun shined brightly through the kitchen window as an indicator that everything would be alright. Brett played with his truck and my pot of coffee smelled great. Although we didn't know the exact location of heaven, one day we would. According to the prayer taught in Matthew 6, heaven is where God resides and He hasn't told Brett (now 26 years old) or me exactly where it is yet.

I'M SORRY,
I THOUGHT YOU SAID HOWARD

This last phrase in the greeting portion of the prayer uses an interesting and rather unique word listed only in the New Testament in Matthew 6 and again in Luke's chapter 11 recording the same prayer. In multitudes of biblical references, a given name has an implied definition characterizing the person with the name. The Bible records name references given not only to people but to places as well, substantiating the importance of a thoughtfully given name.

> "Hallowed be your name."

Unfortunately, today many names are haphazardly doled out due to whims of the parents or relatives with little or no regard given to the possible ramifications of a poorly chosen name. We have all heard stories of terrible names designated to unknowing, vulnerable children. Sometimes, a name is later found out to mean something diametrically opposed to the beliefs and attributes of the person sporting the unfortunate label and in some cases, a legal change is carried out. But from a biblical standpoint, naming a person is a serious issue and should be done with forethought.

As previously stated, numerous names are given in reference to God in the Old Testament, with each name representing His various attributes, power, and glory. In the Matthew 6 prayer, "Hallowed" further clarifies the adoration and reverence of the name by which we address God by stating "Hallowed is Your name." Definitions for "Hallowed," according to *Strong's Exhaustive Concordance* are "to make holy, purify or consecrate," directly relating to some of the characteristics of the Heavenly Father listed in scripture.

So far, in the first two lines of the prayer, the personal aspect of our Father is addressed and defined along with the name of the place of His residence, indicating He is not of earthly origin. The word "Hallowed" is used as an indication of the holiness of His name, by ascribing purity and consecration to even the name by which He is addressed. The initial opening portion of this prayer is indeed a respectfully appropriate greeting and verbal fanfare to our most holy, pure, and consecrated God.

Coming Main Attraction

"Your kingdom come" appears to be a prophetic statement predicting the coming of the long-awaited complete Kingdom of God in full operation here on the earth. Some would argue that the "Kingdom" is already here in part and operating in the lives of those believers living as witnesses to the consciousness of the indwelling Spirit of Christ. Jesus, in Matthew 6:33, taught, "But seek first the Kingdom of God and His righteousness, and all these things shall be added to you." Note that the Kingdom is the first priority in the line of what is to be sought out, as God forever inhabits His Kingdom and the Kingdom does not exist without God's presence. The "things" noted in the scripture are earthly needs and physical concerns. But the Kingdom of God is clearly spiritual and the term "righteousness" is commonly defined as right standing with God. Taking the liberty to paraphrase the verse of Matthew 6:33, we find: Seek before anything else in your life, whether physical or spiritual, the kingdom of God and commit to right standing with Him. Then as a result,

> "Your kingdom come. Your will be done On earth as it is in heaven"

all the other things will be given as seen appropriate by Him.

The statement, "Your will be done on earth as it is in heaven," indicates the coming of God's plan and intent for earth in its fullness and peace. "Will" is defined in this application as "a determination, choice, purpose, decree." As written in the latter portion of Revelation, this will occur in its completion during a future time that is certainly not presently happening. Any national or globally televised newscasts or world events section of a major newspaper confirms the chaotic point of our present time without question. God's will, being accomplished globally as it now is in heaven is obviously not here…yet. However, His will is being fulfilled in part through the body of practicing believers in residence here and now. But it is not until Christ returns to the earth at the end of this age as prophesied in Zachariah 14, and again in Revelation 19, that the kingdom of God will begin its reign in totality on the earth. When His holy will, His determination, His choice, purpose, and His decree become universal on this earth-plane with the same obedience and completion that it is now accomplished in heaven, this scripture will be fulfilled, but not until the appointed time known only to the Father. Biblical prophecy up until the present time is one hundred percent correct, making it a logical slam dunk to assume that it will continue to follow the plan detailed by Jesus recorded in Matthew, Mark, Luke, and far too many other prophets and references to list here. The fulfillment will occur as planned and God's Kingdom and will shall reign just as the prayer states.

A local secular radio and television personality some years ago made it no secret that he believed in the earthly return of Jesus. We became friends after he invited me to discuss biblical end-time prophecy on his drive time radio talk show. The more information and scriptural references I related during the shows, the more interested he became and the more time he'd give me on the next broadcast. As a result of the interest in the subject, the phones at the station rang off the hook, and generally speaking, that is what talk radio is all about...public interest. On the final show I did with him, he gave me the entire two and a half hour show without interruption by call-ins to teach about the coming of Christ. I considered that instance a miracle, considering the secular nature of the station and that the show aired during prime drive time. Each day at the end of his show, he signed off by stating, "If you're living your life as if there is no God... you'd better be right." Ed's sign off echoed this proclamation of God's inevitable reign not only in heaven but on earth as well. Not long ago, Ed went to live in the heavenly kingdom he was so fascinated by, and now he knows all about it, first-hand.

> "If you're living your life as if there is no God... you'd better be right."

Supper Time

It is not until verse 11, approximately mid-point in the structure of this prayer that the theme addresses physical provisions, where human needs are introduced into the petition. Protocol in this prayer by Jesus dictates that acknowledgement of the Father and awareness of His relation to His children should first be recognized and addressed. His holiness, purity, and consecration are glorified with his name referred to as "Hallowed." The fact that His kingdom and ultimate will, as it now exists in heaven, will reign over the earth is professed. It is only after these fundamental spiritual points are acknowledged that our individual physical needs enter into the prayer structure. Please notice use of the word "needs," not to be confused with "wants." The only similarity in the two words is that both contain five letters, which is where the minimal kinship ends. In our materialistically-oriented world, ideas concerning needs are commonly misconstrued and often mistakenly confused with wants. Thankfully, our Heavenly Father is merciful and understands our human shortcomings and spiritual oversights even more than we understand and tolerate the imperfections in our own

> *"Give us this day our daily bread."*

46

evolving children. We should always be thankful for His mercy, which is in itself an ever-present and ongoing need.

"Give us this day our daily bread" is situated in the part of the prayer where our human needs should be properly placed. Take note of the word "give," alluding to the idea that the sustenance is to be consumed or used up, not borrowed to be returned. The bread, or "dole" in some translations, is to be given on "this day" for consumption and will be given on following days to come, hinting at the idea of daily faith required for daily supply, hence the description "daily bread." It should be noted here, according to Old Testament accounts, the provisions of manna provided for the Israelites during the 40-year desert wanderings were also given on a daily regimen with the Sabbath excluded. Manna could not to be hoarded for use at a later time, with the exception of the day before the Sabbath. According to Exodus 16 the manna would breed worms overnight and developed an odor. It would melt in the sun if kept for a later time, with the exception

> "This is the bread which the Lord has given you to eat. This is the thing which the Lord has commanded: "Let every man gather it according to each one's need, one omer for each person according to the number of persons; …But some of them left part of it until morning, and it bred worms and stank …And when the sun became hot, it melted."
> Exodus chapter 16

Michael T. Abadie

of manna gathered a day ahead to be consumed on the Sabbath. The Old Testament story of the Israelites' daily provision could be reflected in the New Testament theme of daily bread recorded in this portion of the prayer. Although the idea is supposition on my part, it does make a thought-provoking correlation.

Another aspect of daily bread comes to light when reading John 6:35. Jesus is again quoted, "I am the bread of life. He who comes to Me shall never hunger, and he who believes in Me shall never thirst." The original Greek word for "bread" is used synonymously in this scripture and in the prayer, thereby posing the possibility that the bread is linked to both physical and spiritual needs. As believers, our physical and spiritual needs are provided for by our Lord at the time they are needed, with faith being the key to the door where the daily bread is kept.

> "According to the law almost all things are purified with blood, and without shedding of blood there is no remission."

At home, Diane and I frequently have personal communion, or what some refer to as "The Lord's Supper," with the customary wine and bread (and yes, we use real wine because Jesus did). We give thanks for healing for ourselves, our children, and our families and friends as we hold the bread before taking it into our bodies. At the last communion before His crucifixion, Jesus gave bread to his disciples and said "this is my body" and instructed them to

48

eat. He then took the cup, gave thanks and said (Matthew 26:28), "For this is my blood of the new covenant which is shed for many for the remission of sins." The reason for the bloodshed for sins is given in Hebrews 9:22, "According to the law almost all things are purified with blood, and without shedding of blood there is no remission." During our communion at home, symbolically as we take the bread or His body, we give thanks for healing and for the physical blessings of provided needs. For it is "by His stripes" and the physical abuse Jesus endured that we are healed in our bodies and the reason we eat the bread in remembrance of the sacrifice. When the wine is taken, symbolizing the shed blood of Christ, in accordance with scripture we give thanks for the spiritual remission of sins by the sacrifice of His blood, and memorialize His death and resurrection for our righteousness or right standing with God.

During our communion, each time we take the bread I am reminded of the daily bread provision in the Lord's Prayer and the provisional gift of manna to those who wandered in the desert. I give thanks that our physical and spiritual needs are provided for on an ongoing daily basis.

ABSOLUTION RESOLUTION

Of all the key words commonly used relating to Christianity, the word "forgive" stands as a verbal monolith underlining the principal and purpose for Jesus' life, death, and resurrection. The definition of the word as used in the New Testament application is to "omit; put away; lay aside." The life, teachings, and ultimate death and resurrection of Jesus became the model for forgiveness and the hope for all humanity. Even while in the incomparable distress of the cross He prayed to the Father to forgive those who put Him there. The descriptive words "debts," "trespasses," and "sins" are used interchangeably in different Bible translations but the terms relate to something owed, a due or fault, an offense or error, and simply *sin,* which is commonly defined as separation from God's will.

> *"And forgive our debts as we forgive our debtors"*

At this juncture, the prayer slightly changes directions and shifts to our spiritual need for alleviation from the weight and burden of our sin, debts, or trespasses common to humanity. According to Paul's epistle in Romans 3:23, "For all have sinned and come short of the glory of God." This verse underscores the corporate need for forgiveness of our transgressions as we all are, or have been, guilty. Old Testament scripture speaks of the absolution of forgiveness in Psalm 103:12, "As far as the east is from the west, so far has He removed our transgressions from us."

> Apparently, our Father does not merely tuck our sins away in a drawer to be pulled out at a later time and shaken in our faces when we mess up again, for that is a human trait.

Apparently, our Father does not merely tuck our sins away in a drawer to be pulled out at a later time and shaken in our faces when we mess up again, for that is a human trait. In short, He loves us unconditionally and He forgives completely.

Personal realization of the joy created by absolution is an indescribable experience and relief. However, the next line of the prayer inserts a stipulation creating for many a monumental roadblock along their spiritual path. According to the wording of the prayer, we are to receive our forgiveness, as or in like manner that we forgive those who are indebted to us, who have offended us, who have erred against us, and so on. Although receiving dispensation is truly a humbling relief, putting the shoe on the other foot to dole out compassion and amnesty is often not easy and many times seems almost impossible to the human psyche. Remember in the first verses of Matthew 6, Jesus came down hard on the social and religious hypocrisy He had witnessed and the concept reappears here concerning the circle of forgiveness. How can we accept forgiveness and not give forgiveness considering that being unforgiving is a sin in itself? In the Kingdom of God, hypocrisy is not tolerated and is considered a serious issue. Simply put, to be forgiven we must also forgive. To receive it, it has to be given. Therein is the bridge or the roadblock.

During an earlier time in my life and as a practicing Christian, I was introduced to a guy who seemed to have some great financial contacts and reportedly could turn a little cash into a whole bunch more within a relatively short amount of time. Stupidly, I grabbed the hook and fell for the "more is better" pitch. After investing a decent amount of cash, I discovered after timely attempts to retrieve my "earnings" that it wasn't readily available at the appointed time. The money I invested had originally come as an unexpected blessing in the form of a bonus and was the only savings to amount to anything I had during that financially embarrassing period of my life. As such, it was desperately needed for upcoming family things and the possibility of increasing the limited amount of resources would have been a great help to pay for the baby on the way. I admit that greed and hope for a greener pasture fueled the initial decision to go for it. But obviously the other guy's greed was greater than mine. His excuses sounded plausible and sincere and I wanted to believe that everything would work out. But it only ended in a seething hatred on my part that chewed at my insides, darkening my days, and resulting in many sleepless nights. I fought the urge to track him down and even thought in terms of bodily harm, but Christians aren't supposed to behave like that. Things of that nature were once a part of my history, but not since I received forgiveness from Christ for my shortcomings. At the time, friends "from the old days" even offered to "take care of it" for me, but that would have been the same as settling the score myself, so I declined the temptation of the offers. Deciding to choose the spiritually correct route, I prayed and prayed for answers but the prayers seemed to bounce right off the walls with no apparent response as weeks turned into months. But on one special night during a humbling prayer time, an inner voice instructed me to pray for the clown who took my money. My first thoughts were that I couldn't bring myself to pray positively for him with the hate I was feeling and even if I did, I would be a super hypocrite for praying something I didn't mean.

> My lips prayed for him. My flesh wanted to kill him.

The inner voice continued with the same message: "Pray for Henry." I finally agreed to pray but only with my disclaimer that the prayer would come from my lips but not my heart and I would need a "hypocrite disclosure" to be understood between the Lord and me in order to do it. Numerous times during the day and at night, I would obediently pray for Henry for his salvation and forgiveness of his sins while feeling like the biggest spiritual fraud in the world. My lips prayed for him. My flesh wanted to kill him. After weeks of Henry prayers, late one evening while in prayer my heart tuned in to the personal anguish he must be feeling by living the life he did. As the strange empathy began to grow, I actually felt his need, his despair, and his need for forgiveness from God. From my heart, this time

I petitioned the Lord for Henry's salvation as tears of earnest compassion washed away the terrible feelings that had plagued me only a short time ago. During the time of my anger, I would never have believed this situation would turn around as it did with a profound plea for the guy who had swindled me. In order to keep this story from becoming another book, I will say in short, that my understanding of the "forgiveness as I forgive" principle became alive and breathed new spiritual understanding into my life. Henry and I were both at fault, and the forgiveness I was mandated to pray for replaced a mountain of ill feelings and inner turmoil. Although I haven't seen Henry in 30-plus years, I still occasionally pray for him and thank God that the roadblock is gone, the bridge is open, and God forgives both of us.

> I personally believe that whether we realize it or not, we are hard wired from our creation to know right from wrong and good from bad.

Medically, it is a known fact that mental stress can ultimately produce physically detrimental side effects. Bitterness, also known as un-forgiveness, has been identified as a major contributor to various physical disorders and mental duress that can take its toll on the whole body. When a person does not truly forgive others, then their own forgiveness is very difficult for them to accept and the goose and the gander come home to roost in a nest of mutual misery. On the other hand, when the realization of the weight of sin is relieved by accepting forgiveness, we are more likely to desire and offer the same amnesty for others. I personally believe that whether we realize it or not, we are hard wired from our creation to know right from wrong and good from bad. Desiring blessings for others as well as for ourselves is a prime example of that positive school of thought. Scripture, directly following the Lord's Prayer in Matthew 6:14-15, states, "For if you forgive men their trespasses, your heavenly Father will also forgive you. But if you do not forgive men their trespasses, neither will your Father forgive your trespasses." This quote from Jesus has been used by many well-meaning people as a sort of threat in an attempt to mandate forgiveness which cannot actually be legislated. As such, it becomes an oxymoron. However, with the understanding of what comprises true forgiveness from the heart, these two lines of the prayer become clearer. No longer viewed as a threat but as a path to mutually enjoyed freedom from transgressions, forgiveness becomes a type of insurance for our own peace of mind. The formerly perceived threat proves to be a glorious plan for blessing as the forgiver becomes the forgiven and the circle is completed.

Although huge numbers of books have been written concerning forgiveness, the power of peace granted to us by granting freedom to others cannot be overstated. It was a very important point to Jesus and is an imperative point for us as we open the doors to the temple within.

Don't Throw Me in the Mudhole

> "And do not lead us into temptation"

For years on end, this line of the prayer threw me a continual curve ball. In the epistle of James 1:13 we find an interesting reassurance concerning the origin of temptation, "Let no one say when he is tempted, I am tempted of God; for God cannot be tempted by evil, **nor does He Himself tempt anyone**." Grasping this confirmation that God does not tempt anyone, why do we pray "do not lead us into temptation" knowing that God scripturally is not supposed to do that? Psalms 5:4 states, "For you are not a God who takes pleasure in wickedness, nor shall evil dwell with You." James 1:14 further clarifies the answer to the question by stating, "But each one is tempted when he is drawn away by his **own desires** and enticed." Man is tempted or enticed when he is "drawn away" by the tempter, but the decision to yield to or resist that temptation is within the free will granted to man by God.

The *Concordant Literal Translation* of the prayer scripture relates "And mayest Thou not be bringing us into trial…" From the original Greek word meaning "trial," further translation renders "temptation." James relates that the temptation comes when a person is drawn away by their **own** desire, thereby removing God from the erroneous position of being the tempter, which He is most certainly not. Scripturally, temptation is generally related to Satan who is also referred to as *the tempter.*

During a prayer time one day, the verse once again prompted the proverbial question. While in the process of prayer, I simply did what I should have done long ago and asked for enlightenment concerning the seemingly paradoxical prayer line. Almost instantly a simple answer came from nowhere. To pray "do not lead us into temptation (or trial)" we are in effect saying "lead us away from temptation." Same idea and end result but with a phrasing adjustment. For instance we could say to someone "do not lead me into that mud hole," or we could say "lead me away from that mud hole," two different phrasings, same meaning and end result. "Lead us away from temptation" clears up my former prayer line issue and also relates the same idea and desired outcome. Without a doubt, our Lord does not lead anyone into temptation, but certainly does lead us away from it. Further punctuating the point, James records in chapter 1, verse 2, "My brethren, count it all joy when you fall into various trials, knowing that the trying of your faith produces patience." I will be the first to admit that joy is never the first thing that comes to my mind when trials descend upon my life. But knowing that particular scripture in James sure helps out, especially when the next verse is brought into the mix, "But let patience have its perfect work, that you may be perfect and complete, lacking nothing." Nevertheless, I tend to ask to be lead **away** from temptation as the prayer states. It is much nicer to be led around the rose bushes than to be pushed through them.

> It is much nicer to be led around the rose bushes than to be pushed through them.

For those readers who may at this time be "rending their garments" thinking this book is an attempt to re-write the Lord's Prayer, rest assured I have only ventured to understand it better on a more comprehensive level and relate to others desiring to pray more effectively. Any prayer that Jesus dictates to His disciples should be understood as completely as possible and was included in His teachings for the express purpose of helping all people to pray properly and effectively.

DEVIL WITHOUT THE "D"

Precisely placed directly after the petition to be kept from temptation, we find a corresponding appeal but this time to be delivered from "the evil one" or simply "evil" as stated in the original King James. The word "deliver" in this context is defined as "to rush or draw, i.e. rescue," or as noted and paraphrased in the previous paragraphs, to be lead away from.

> "But deliver us from the evil one"

How better to avoid temptation than to be led away from the one identified as the tempter. The idea today that there is really no "evil one" or "Satan" that actually exists is a convenient way to avoid an unpleasant and unpopular issue. If Satan did not exist, then who was it that tempted Jesus in the desert? Who was it that Jesus had words with there and defeated with the truth and power of the word of God? In the book of Revelation, chapter 20 verse 2 states, "He laid hold of the dragon, that serpent of old who is the Devil and Satan, and bound him for a thousand years." If this evil one does not exist, then why does our most sacred book of scripture acknowledge his existence throughout? In the Old Testament there are far too many verses to list here that contain phrases such as "the Lord said unto

Satan," "Satan answered the Lord," and "Satan came also among them," and so on as scripture after scripture reveals. Jesus taught in the Lord's Prayer that we should desire deliverance, or translated as "rescue" from this evil one. Unfortunately, the deception that Satan is no more than our own imagination or self-centered alter-ego has taken hold in the secular world and has even infiltrated, to a degree, some Christian denominations. Fictitious non-existence causing the prey to believe the enemy isn't there is a very effective battle tactic. Through "non-existence" or invisibility, the attacker is no longer a perceived threat and may wage covert assaults at will with little or no resistance. Being commonly relegated as a mere cartoon character further lessens the idea of an actual threat.

As the prayer is recorded in the book of Luke chapter 11, this verse brings it to an end. However in Matthew chapter 6 record of the prayer, we find the additional doxology discussed in the next chapter of this book.

PROMINENCE, PLACE, POWER, AND PRAISE

> *"For Yours is the kingdom and the power and the glory forever"*

This final proclamation closely resembles a portion of prayer recorded in the Old Testament in 1 Chronicles 29:11. It was offered by King David as thanksgiving for gifts provided for the Temple. David, a blood relative of Jesus, 28 generations before, prayed:

"Yours, O Lord, is the greatness, the power and the glory. The victory and the majesty;

For all that is in heaven and in the earth is Yours;

Yours is the kingdom, O Lord, and You are exalted as head over all."

The final sentence of the Lord's Prayer in Matthew 6 provides an appropriate finish of praise and recognition to our hallowed, holy, all powerful God, exalted above heaven and earth. The Kingdom is His because without Him the Kingdom does not exist. The One who created the Universe and everything in it is without a doubt the all-powerful One. He who creates also possesses the capability to destroy, denoting another aspect of the power in His possession. The One we call God is the heavenly sovereign Father, creator of our humanity, who cares for us without preference, as no mortal soul fully understands. How humbling it is to know the omnipotent Creator of all that is, ever was, and all that will be, hears our petitions, provides us protection and provisions for our sustenance, and allows our heartfelt prayers into His throne room. As the unchanging eternal ruler and ultimate majesty, to whom belongs the Kingdom, He concerns Himself with us. In the first words of the prayer, we are allowed to greet Him personally as "Our Father." At the end of this prayer we declare His glory, dignity, honor, praise, and worship, forever.

PLANT THE SEED, REAP THE DEED

Throughout recorded history mankind has witnessed innumerable arrangements of patterns occurring naturally in humans, animals, the earth and sea, as well as in the rest of creation. Even casual observations of the world and the people around us readily reveal that many occurrences are also a result of cyclical or patterned arrangements. The Bible records examples of patterns in human behavior, particularly in mankind's relationship with God. The Old Testament writings contain account after account of man living in peace and prospering while obeying God's law and living according to His will. Sooner or later, man's own will or ego rises up as an affront to God's presence in attempts to live in separation from God. The peace and prosperity predictably turns to war and poverty as man sinks into the pit of spiritual separation otherwise known as sin. After the lesson is learned,

> Patterns are everywhere, as history teaches, and extended operation contrary to the predictable arrangements always end in some form of calamity.

mankind turns its head toward right standing in obedience to God, and once again finds the road to peaceful abundance. Jesus' life and His teachings existed as and professed patterns of thought, belief, actions, and outcomes. Many of these truths were taught within the context of the parables recorded in the gospels. The parables were taught as patterns of probable outcomes directly proportional to the input possibilities. Nature itself teaches that apple seeds planted will produce apples and only apples. Tomato seeds will produce only tomatoes and not anything else. From the standpoint of humanity, negative human behaviors result in negative outcomes and energies, while positive inputs and behaviors result in positive rewards from the resultant positive energy. Eastern philosophies teach precepts of yin and yang, inflow and outflow of positive and negative life force energies, as do other similar ideologies. Although outcomes are sometimes painfully slow to materialize by human perception of time standards, results will always bear the likeness of the seed planted, because the eventual result of pattern implementation is in itself an unchangeable pattern.

Patterns are quite prevalent in our daily lives and serve to teach us lessons of divinely orchestrated order. Unfortunately, chaotic disorder rampant in countless places throughout the world is also patterned behavior, well documented in our written and visual news publications. Patterns and habits, though similar, should never be confused as the same thing. Divinely designed patterns cannot be changed and always prevail, while habitual actions can be adjusted, and in some cases should absolutely be revised. Negative personal habits, frequently unrecognized by the person displaying the disposition, almost always develop into unfavorable outcomes, and if allowed to persist, can evolve into repetitive destructive

> "Hear and understand," Jesus stated, "Not what goes into the mouth defiles a man; but what comes out of the mouth, this defiles a man" Matthew 15:11.

life patterns. By letting go of counterproductive habits and concentrating focus on the intended beneficial outcome, a person can switch tracks and position themselves into a positive life pattern which tends to reproduce in like manner. The idea can be summed up in the much quoted adage that continually doing the same things and expecting a different outcome is insanity defined.

When confronted by Pharisees with questions regarding the issue of traditional hand washing by the disciples and lack of some habitual religious practices, Jesus answered by referring to the Pharisees as "hypocrites" (Matthew 15:7). He followed with the statement "Well did Isaiah prophesy about you," and quoted from Isaiah 29:13,

> *"Inasmuch as these people draw near with their mouths,*
> *And honor me with their lips,*
> *But have removed their hearts far from Me,*
> *And their fear toward Me is taught by the*
> *commandments of men."*

It can be surmised from Jesus' answer to the outwardly pious religious leaders of the day that traditions and commandments "of men" had become shallow, patterned, and habitual temple practices to be heard and seen by those within earshot but actually driven by insincere egotistical intentions. Again the point is revisited by the Son of God that the intent of the spiritual heart is the true measure of a person, not the vain endeavor of baseless words. Jesus echoed the position of righteousness (or right standing with God) in His "Sermon on the Mount" recorded in Matthew 5:20, "For I say to you, that unless your righteousness exceeds the righteousness of the scribes and Pharisees, you will by no means enter the kingdom of heaven." It's easy to see His opinion of the Pharisees' practices was one of disrespect even to the point of intimating they missed the boat concerning the true values of worship and a personal relationship with God. The saying "old habits die hard" correctly fits the situation of the manmade temple rituals as the spiritually "elite" turned a deaf ear to the teachings of Jesus. They would later accuse Him of blaspheming God and complain that He challenged traditional ritual, primarily doctrines of men, and threatened the status quo. Patterned negative behaviors have a way of landing us square in the middle of the crop we have planted, with that same crop being the only thing on the menu for a long time. If the yield of the produce is to our liking, then it's all the better. But if we have produced what we don't care for, it may be time to learn the lesson and replant what tastes good.

At this point, it is made clear why Jesus taught the disciples and those listening to pray in a different way, not from a ceremonial prearranged habitual recitation and "not in a vain and repetitious manner," but directly from the heart to the ears of the Father. The prayer is addressed to "Our Father," demonstrating that God is willing to hear from all His children personally as a loving parent on a personalized individual basis. Communication with our God is the most holy significant and reverent utterance we are privileged to practice. With that in mind, it is important to follow a respectful protocol. The prayer taught by Jesus provides the framework, or pattern of a perfectly designed model prayer constructed in order of importance for us to humbly present before God, Our Father.

OUR FATHER, HIS FATHER, MY FATHER

Streets in the neighborhood were dark and quiet with only the occasional night sounds breaking the silence as I walked in prayer on a very special night years ago. Stars were visible in the sky between the evenly-spaced street lights that outshined the tiny florescence glistening from light years away. Although having developed a close and cherished relationship with my Lord and Savior years before, prayers under the lengthy emotional distress of that time had grown stale and had begun to all sound

> I seemed to be stuck in my own mud and couldn't gain traction enough to find a way out.

the same. I seemed to be stuck in my own mud and couldn't gain traction enough to find a way out. During the course of the average work day, numerous conversations with my clients along with the focus of helping others with their own problems became a welcome diversion from my own ever-present issues. As a coping mechanism, I had learned to stuff the disruptions of my own life into a secret mental closet behind a tightly shut door, only to be opened during the privacy of my nightly prayer time. For the previous few prayer walks, I had attempted to mostly remain silent and listen in order to practice the "be still" admonition of Psalms 46:10. I hoped this difference in routine and change of technique would put an end to the "help me" prayers that had grown far too familiar.

On that "special" night, I remember just leveling with the Lord, man to man, or more correctly, "man to God," and confessing that I didn't know what to pray anymore and I would depend on the prayer Jesus taught to maybe shed some light on my deepening personal darkness. As stated in a previous chapter, the initial greeting of "Our Father, who is in heaven" came forth and I was prompted to stop and think about what I had just said, word by word.

Maybe the stillness could help me to listen between the phrases for the connection I had yet to grasp. Maybe I could tune in to what was being preached from the temple within. Maybe it was what had been lacking and maybe that's where the peace could be found. Wouldn't that take the cake if the prayer I had known since childhood contained some answers for me 30-something years later and almost (at that time) 2000 years after it was taught by Jesus!

"Our Father"

As the first word of the prayer, "Our," came from my lips, I was reminded that Jesus also referred to God as "Father." The scripture in John 14:28 came to mind where Jesus said "I am going to my Father for my Father is greater than I." "Our Father" indicates that Jesus and I, along with all others, do in fact have the same Father, in affect making us spiritual family members. The importance of the word "our" in that initial prayer opening is a powerful concept that makes the terminology "Father" even more personal.

"Father"—I was only on the second word of the prayer being prayed in this different way and the lights of understanding were already starting to glow. Having heard the point preached in numerous pulpit messages, I was aware that God loves us even more than any earthly father could imagine. Even though I am a father, my thoughts immediately jumped a generation to my own dad. I always knew without a shadow of a doubt that as a boy my dad would protect me from whatever may come, and into adulthood his advice and support from a guys' point of view was always there for me. Even when my ideas and actions were wrong, he would wisely lead me back to the path of doing the right thing at the right time, with the admonition of *"If you'd just do what you're supposed to do, when you're supposed to do it, things would work out a lot better."* His tone was stern, his logic was solid, and his love was steadfast. My thoughts reverted back to the time of a milestone during my late teens. Due to my hardheaded, rebellious nature in the late 60's, the fabric of the relationship with my dad had become torn. After vowing not to set foot in their house again, Mom called me after some time had passed and asked if I would come over to have coffee with her and talk while Dad was at work. After I ranted and raved about how narrow-minded and ridiculous I thought Dad had become, Mom calmly said,

"Let me tell you something about your dad. Remember when that notice came from the draft board concerning the military physical, and you thought the military may draft

you into service? And remember how Dad never liked to talk much about World War II, the Battle of the Bulge, and D-Day at Normandy? He would never say very much on the subject because after he had to do what he did as a paratrooper on "special missions" with all the kill or be killed stuff, the death and destruction, he didn't want to think about all that he'd seen and done. After all the years, he still has nightmares about it and sometimes he wakes up with tears in his eyes calling out the names of his buddies. He hated the idea of war and killing. Here's the point: when that notice came in the mail for you, it really affected your dad. Without any of us knowing what he was doing, he went to the Army recruiter and offered himself in your place, making the case that he was already trained and had seen everything a man in a war could see and that it would be far more logical for them to take him instead. He took the two Purple Hearts and some of his other medals with him to prove the point. Knowing how much he hated war and everything that went with it, he would rather go through it all again than to see you have to do it. Of course the age factor kept it from becoming a reality, but your dad would have definitely gone in your place." Mom said, *but I figured that you needed to know how much your dad really loves you and he would give his life to save yours without question."*

Needless to say, the strain between my dad and me disappeared quickly as I rediscovered that I loved him after all, and now I knew he never stopped loving me. Even during my periodic craziness, Dad, with Mom at his side, was always there for me, even when I didn't know it. Many years later in his early 80s, he was diagnosed with terminal lung cancer caused by asbestos exposure, and once again he fought a brave and intense battle. I spoke of the love he showed to Mom, my brother Kevin, and me as I preached his funeral. Family stories were recounted, and we watched a DVD of a local news story a television station had done about him. But mere words could never tell the whole saga during the allotted and limited time of a funeral tribute. He was our *Dad of Dads* and our earthly superhero who had gone on permanent vacation before the rest of us. My earthly father is now in the presence of our heavenly Father, and in due time, we will all be together again, and as I promised, I'll see you there, Dad!

> *"I wasn't supposed to ever say anything about it and your dad doesn't need to know I told you,'*

Knowing the intensity and strength of a parent's love, it is unimaginable from the perspective of a mortal mind that my heavenly Father loves us even more. I can't fully comprehend it but I know it's true. Jesus started the prayer with "**Our** Father." That same heavenly Father sent a vitally important part of himself to experience mortal death so that we all may have an eternal life free of the burden of sin. Our Savior verified in John

> "If anyone loves Me, he will keep my word; and My Father will love him, and We will come to him and make Our home with him."

14:9 that He and the Father are one when He told Philip, "He who has seen Me has seen the Father." In John 14:23, Jesus further makes the point of spiritual unity with the believer, "If anyone loves Me, he will keep my word; and My Father will love him, and We will come to him and make Our home with him."

The "Father" in the prayer from that night on, was still "Our Father," but it felt alright to address Him more personally as "my Father" as I still do when I pray. I don't think the Lord minds this slight deviation from the original as it is correct from a scriptural point of view. The opening words of the Lord's Prayer were revealed to be so much more than the simple greeting I had previously prayed before the enlightenment, and I thanked my heavenly Father for the revelation as I walked on through the neighborhood streets.

HOW MANY YEARS ARE IN FOREVER?

After a time of stillness, I prayed *"Who is in heaven"* with anticipation of what was about to be revealed.

Thoughts revolving around the concept of heaven began to swirl around in my mind as questions about the subject materialized. Heaven is commonly thought of as a place far removed from where we are. Or is it? Where is this mystical residence where God exists and rules that is even contemplated by four-year-olds, and where He is accompanied by other beings unlike anything we experience here in this earthly realm? Death is sometimes referred to as "passing" or "crossing over." "Passing" to what or "crossing over" to where? Going to live with God is often the vague answer for what we do not understand concerning death for lack of more detailed information. I believe heaven is apparently a place that exists irrelevant to the constraints of time and relative space as we know it. As an

> Death is sometimes referred to as "passing" or "crossing over." "Passing" to what or "crossing over" to where?

eternal being, God's continuance is without end, and that may be, to some extent, almost feasible to earthly finite reasoning. However, God has apparently existed forever and as an eternal being without beginning or end, has never had a "start point" or relative birthday as all created things share in common. My human understanding of existing forever, although abstract, can almost be grasped; almost. But the thought of having existed forever without a beginning is where my human reasoning falls off the cliff of feasibility. God has existed forever, so the place which He inhabits must also have existed forever. And that place of Holy infinite energy is called "heaven," as confirmed by the Lord's Prayer, among many other Biblical references.

I attempted to imagine being free of the confinement of time as we know it, but the thoughts kept ending up at the end of a mental circle because our very lives and everything relative to them are attached to a time frame. There is a possibility that heaven could be as close as the air we breathe or even closer, as the spaces between the atoms that we are made of and the energy that gives them functionality. And what about the spaces between the planets and the energy force there that keeps them in their orbits. Could all of that be portions of heaven which is the energy of God's presence that holds everything together?

There are hundreds, even thousands of intelligible frequencies intercepted by our televisions and receiving devices, but we're only aware of the precise channel we are tuned to at any given time. It's also a fact that innumerable frequencies are present on and around the earth with vibrations or frequencies also emanating from parts of the Universe within range of our perception and reception. In a comparison of heaven and earth, mortal life seems to be tuned to a different channel or frequency of comprehension. Is it possible that heaven might exist all around us and even inside us, and at the same time, on a different frequency to which we're not yet tuned to fully perceive? Could it be that "passing away" or "crossing over" at the end of mortality is a change of frequency or simply changing the life channel?

> Is it possible that heaven might exist all around us and even inside us, and at the same time, on a different frequency to which we're not yet tuned to fully perceive?

One thing I do believe is that You my Father, inhabit a place called heaven that I can postulate but really can't comprehend. But one day we all will have first-hand experience as the veil is parted and I thank you for that anticipation.

I am grateful, Lord God that you are my Father and that heaven belongs to you and contains many places there prepared for us as Jesus promised.

After that part of the prayer, I walked on in silence for a while as some "still time" was needed to consider the possibilities of the eternal place I would be blessed to experience one day.

THE NAME, THE KINGDOM, AND THE BREAD

At the beginning of the prayer I addressed God as "our Father" and after some reflection it felt good and far more personal to call Him "my Father." But praying and contemplating through the structure of this part of the prayer, "Hallowed" is brought to the forefront. I am reminded that biblical names, unlike many names today, were given for the purpose of a description of the person bearing the name. Numerous times a person's name, along with the accompanying description, was revised to more accurately reflect a change in their life or purpose attached to their mission. In my adolescence someone once told me that my name, Michael, meant "messenger of God." During my teens and into my early adulthood, I occasionally brought that up at parties as a joke, and everybody laughed because they knew the way I lived and at that time in my life, I was certainly not a fulfillment of the name I was given. I don't joke about that anymore and do not take the idea of my name lightly.

At this point in the prayer it seemed correct to pray *"Father, even your name is Hallowed"* from a standpoint of praise and even celebration of the holy purity of His consecrated countenance. In actuality, mere words seem to be a feeble attempt to describe a one-of-a-kind, ultimately powerful but loving Supreme Being. However, words, emotions, and certain actions and inactions (such as being still before Him) are all I have to convey love and respect to Him. Words, although mortal, do have the ability to reach into heavenly realms according to what I read in the Bible about prayers. There are indeed some words I have spoken that I wish I could erase, but they tend to live on as words do. Fortunately, even words that we regret are forgiven by our Lord, who is also known (ironically) as the Word.

> Once spoken aloud, the essence of our words becomes alive and can never be erased, whether used as tools of communication or even as weapons.

But you, O Lord, know the intents of my heart, my strengths, and my flaws, along with the regret I feel for irreverently spoken words that I can't erase.

With that in mind, I choose carefully the words I speak to You and I choose words of praise, honor, and edification. You, however, are most Hallowed to the point that your name is a word reflective of an integral part of your nature and will be celebrated along with your many other names for all eternity. You are described with a multitude of given names, yet as God, you need none.

"Your kingdom come"

"Your will be done on earth as it is in heaven."

Having studied Biblical and particularly end-time prophecy for years, this part of the prayer revealed to me the prophecy of the coming fullness of the Kingdom of God upon this earth. For some reason, until now I had not seen this prayer line for what it is. At the culmination of this present age at the end of the tribulation period, Jesus will return to reign as the Prince of Peace from the millennial, or thousand year, Kingdom, seated in Israel, according to the book of Revelation.

Father, I am aware of the prophecies and promises of Your Holy Kingdom coming to reign in majesty and universal consciousness on this earth and I rejoice at the thought. I know Jesus said (in Luke 17:21) the Kingdom of God is within us or translated "in our midst," and I am grateful that even now we are not separated from you. The indwelling of Your Kingdom in this earthly vessel is an example for complete fulfillment in the whole of the earth. Thank you Lord that Your Kingdom will certainly come and Your will shall be accomplished not only in the Heavenly Kingdom but upon this earth as well.

Father, I feel that this generation is so very blessed to be living in this time segment when we are allowed to witness so many prophecies coming to fruition that were given even thousands of years ago. Thank you, Lord, that I, like so many others, believe the end of this age is at hand and your return is near.

"Give us this day our daily bread"

At this point, I am reminded of the bread given to the disciples by Jesus at the Passover, or actually what could be looked upon as the first communion given shortly before His crucifixion. Without a doubt, they must have had a hard time understanding what Jesus was conveying to them. As He said "Take, eat; this is My body," some of them must have silently questioned His words. As they drank from the wine cup, Jesus told them it was His blood, shed for the remission of sins. It was probably at that point where the light of understanding for some of them began to slowly illuminate and the symbolism began to paint a partial picture of what the near future held in store.

That "bread," O Lord, that precious body of Jesus, endured the cruelty and the viciousness inflicted upon Him, all to bear the sacrifice in Himself for us so that our redemption could be purchased. During the times of the Old Testament law, the shedding of blood was taken from sacrificed animals by the priests for the benefit of the people. But at the advent of this New Testament, or New Covenant, it became your body and blood that was given to atone for the sins of the Jew and Gentile alike and for all who would accept your sacrifice in the future. I am grateful that you are no respecter of persons and that all of humankind has been created equally. Although occurring 2000 or so years ago, your blameless body and blood was given in payment for my sins and for the sins of all on a daily regimen as needed. Help me to remember all this when temptation attempts to stand between us.

And Father I am ever mindful of the daily physical sustenance and for the healing of our bodies provided by you with boundless mercy and grace. We are administered all spiritual and physical needs by You that we may have life more abundantly according to Your words in scripture. Thank you for these gifts and benefits and for the provision of our spiritual and physical daily bread.

FORGIVE, FORGIVEN, FORGIVING

"And forgive us our debts, trespasses, or sins
As we forgive our debtors who have trespassed or sinned
against us"

The people who have lived in forms of bondage are the ones who are most aware of its demands and constraints and are also the ones who have the greatest appreciation for the freedom to choose when given the opportunity. From a spiritual viewpoint, the sinners who have been the greatest offenders of the laws of God's love are the very souls who are the most grateful for the abolition of their sins from the moment of salvation.

> From the self-imposed valley, the beauty of the mountaintop in the distance was well within view but getting there seemed less than a remote possibility.

In my "former life" (before salvation), I was guilty of many offenses before God. So much so that for some time I honestly believed that I had done far too much to be forgiven. Certainly, He would not simply erase all that I had done and even if it could happen, I could never pay enough penance by whatever means to cover the sins committed against Him. During those dark times, I honestly thought my miserable fate had been nailed shut and sealed by me for all eternity. From the self-imposed valley, the beauty of the mountaintop in the distance was well within view but getting there seemed less than a remote possibility. Thankfully, a pastor named David took the time to explain the extent and scope of God's love and forgiveness in a manner that I could partially understand and actually believe was possible. Although I don't care to talk much about or glorify those "bad years" before salvation, sometimes when a person I am speaking with concerning spiritual forgiveness is under the same misconception as I was, I share a bit of my history in order to exhibit the mercy and faithfulness of God. By that type of rare witness, I am always humbled to see that even my most blatant sins can be used to further the awareness of blessed forgiveness paid for by the blood of a Savior on a rough-hewn cross.

Father, the gratitude I feel for the blessing of forgiveness is overwhelming. Your mercy is shown to me every waking hour of my life. I do not ask again for the forgiveness you have already given but I am in continual thankfulness for it every moment of each day. Each morning as I see my reflection in the mirror, I look upon a face of one who has been forgiven of a multitude of sins. I gaze upon a person who has been made whole again and healed from the deathly disease of unbelief and separation from my Creator. Words are not adequate to express the gratitude and joy you have allowed me to experience in the freedom from spiritual oppression in which I once lived due to ignorance of your provisions. Thank you that I now live and will forever live in your Kingdom and that Your Spirit dwells within me. Although the past was a definite reality, by mercy it has been washed from me and now lives only in a faint memory that I do not dwell on except in thanks for having been removed from it.

Because of the extent of my forgiveness, you have allowed me to see myself in those who sin or trespass against me. As I see them in my "mirror," I am able to forgive in the manner that I was and am still forgiven. By passing the mercy that You have given me to others, it continues to become even larger in the sight of all who have formerly lived in the bondage of sin. Father, I am grateful for the freedom of forgiveness I have received and for the freedom and forgiveness you have allowed me to share. In the manner that I have been forgiven, is the manner in which I can now forgive, and because I forgive, I am forgiven.

STEER ME CLEAR

"And lead me away from temptation" (From scripture, "And do not lead us into temptation")

"But deliver us from the evil one"

Lord, in accordance with the words of 1 John 4:4, I confess the scripture "He who is in you (in this case me) is greater than he who is in the world." By that truth, victory over the whiles of Satan can be declared by the power of Your Spirit and by Your abiding and directing presence within me. I am grateful that You, O Lord, lead me away from temptation and have protected me from the grasp and influence of the tempter, also known as the evil one. Provide us with sharp discernment so that we may not be deceived by false prophets. Father, I do ask that You strengthen me to keep my eyes and my heart set upon things of the Spirit and that the things of this world continue to grow dim in comparison to the light of Your countenance. As the words of 2 Corinthians 4:18 state, "For the things which are seen are temporal

> As the words of 2 Corinthians 4:18 state, "For the things which are seen are temporal (or temporary), but the things which are not seen are eternal."

(or temporary), but the things which are not seen are eternal." Help us to keep focused upon the currently invisible things of the spirit. Help us to see them with the vision of our hearts while keeping the earthly visible and tangible things in the temporary light in which they should be perceived. It is comforting to know Your Word in the book of Psalms speaks of the angels that have been given charge over us to keep and protect us in all our ways.

Thank you Father, for Your guidance to steer us away from evil and for protection from the evil one.

ONLY YOU

"For Yours is the Kingdom and the power and the glory forever" You O God, possess not only the Kingdom that is within but also the Kingdom that is the all of everything. It is the essence of You, as is Your residence within it. You and you alone are the almighty King and Lord over all. You are the epitome of supreme power and possess the authority to create or to destroy in order to recreate that which pleases you. The power of Your countenance can not be understood or measured by human understanding but one day will be known, experienced, and seen by all. The power of Your unconditional love is a universal beacon of hope to mortals who have difficulty understanding the concept of true love. As God, you can only be love because you are love in its purest form. Your glory has shown forever and will continue as a light of guidance into the vastness of timeless eternity. Who but You, O Lord, can be called "Glorious"? Forever is a term we recognize, but fail to fully understand due to the nature of our finite minds. But I

> The only words of true gratitude I can express seem far too few and lack the eloquence that would seem to be needed.

know that we will, at the chosen time, understand with the revealing of your enlightenment. I continue to marvel that an infinite God loves me and hears my prayers, heals my body, and sends comfort to my soul from the temple within. The only words of true gratitude I can express seem far too few and lack the eloquence that would seem to be needed. Considering all these things, I humbly say "Thank you" for all you are and for saving me that I may worship you in gratitude forever. As David recorded in the Psalms, I can also say "I will live in the house of the Lord forever." I am grateful to God, Our Father...My Father who is in heaven.

THANKS FOR THE GRATITUDE

We have all been told on innumerable occasions by our loved ones, pastors, priests, and others to count our blessings in order to help us see beyond ourselves and our immediate problems during times of trouble or distress. I do understand that when difficult times arrive at our doorstep and attempt to homestead there, personal focus can easily become tuned to the negative energy carried with the unwelcome visitor. I relate to this issue personally from having been there many times. By "tuning in" and attaching our countenance to the negatives, we create a form of attachment and add fuel to the fire that is burning at our own feet. Usually as the issue builds in our mind, we seem to add to the problem by allowing our overactive imagination to build entire mountain ranges out of the proverbial mole hill camped on the welcome mat. At this point, the advice of

> By "tuning in" and attaching our countenance to the negatives, we create a form of attachment and add fuel to the fire that is burning at our own feet.

counting of blessings is very hard to appreciate due to the momentum already in process brought on by the human fascination with negative thought patterns and pointless internal conversations. Yes, I did say fascination, and the statement is truer than we like to admit.

The fact is that modern society does have a growing fixation upon negative emotions, imaginations, and actions. Proof of the statement is easy to substantiate by simply listening to open conversations between friends, office mates, and family members to find out what the latest point of interest revolves around. The most popular news broadcasts are filled with primarily negatively-oriented stories because the old adage that *negative news sells* is proven day after day. The most celebrated movies and television shows filling the living rooms of the world are filled with violence of all degrees. It seems as if every actor has to have a gun out of the holster and pointed at someone else with an equally bad attitude, and blood puddles of the victims are the teasers for the next episodes. We have to be careful not to put all the blame on the producers because they only create what the public wants to watch. The latest electronic games sold by the millions are war-related or crime-oriented, with car chases, crashes, and explosions accented with bullet-riddled bodies paving the streets. The games are highlighted by who causes more destruction by killing the most and who gains the most points for doing so. Just a quick run through the channel selections and the movie and game ads will prove the point without question. The real story here is that a huge part of life as we know it, and even what has come to be known as entertainment, many times revolves around the most negative of scenarios with the public paying hard-earned cash to see even more. It is quite easy to understand how negativity is allowed to maintain such a firm grip on a large part of the population that will stand in line to feed the beast that eats the soul.

Paul and Timothy's letter to the Philippians outlines a number of things that should be meditated on—things which are noble, just, pure, lovely, of a good report, virtuous, and praiseworthy. All of which are positive and constructive. In all the "things" listed to be dwelled upon, negativity is nowhere to be found. The fact that negative energy exists in close proximity to all of us is irrefutable. However, we are given the choice and the free will to allow ourselves to be drawn to it or to walk away from it. By reading through the teachings of Jesus and His instructions for the coming generations, it becomes clear to the reader that somewhere along the line, something went wrong and public attention tuned to another channel sponsored by a much lower form of energy. While evident that Jesus did teach about some of the terrible things that would happen during the tribulation at the end of this age, He noted that we should focus on the positive blessings and redemption fueled by faith in the good news of His earthly coming and His

> Somewhere along the line, something went wrong and public attention tuned to another channel sponsored by a much lower form of energy.

present indwelling of the believers. He taught of joy in the 15th chapter of John, "so that My joy may remain in you, and that your joy may be full." He taught about the gravity and importance of love by stating, "This is my commandment that you love one another as I have loved you." In the very next chapter, alluding to His death and resurrection, He promised to send us "another Comforter" or "Helper," also known as the Holy Spirit, to assist and comfort our hearts in a much closer personal relationship. "Ask and you will receive, that your joy may be full" (John 16:24) is good news in anybody's book.

Apparently in order to dwell in joy and the peace of the spirit, the believer should live a positively charged lifestyle (known as faith) and stay a safe distance from the clutches of chaos so prevalent in today's world system if at all possible. "Lead us not into temptation" can be translated as lead us away from the things we should not be around. By wisely associating ourselves with those positive spiritual things, our focus can be redirected toward the light of the spirit and away from the darkness that loves nothing more than an increase in its proliferation. Even well-meaning practicing Christians can be drawn into the web of negativity. Positive and negative "vibrations" are energetic entities and tend to reproduce after their own kind. The true essence of peace is a witness of positive energy and the resulting indwelling joy. Paul states in Colossians 3:15, "And let the peace of God rule in your hearts." Notice that Paul wrote the word "rule" and not "periodically visit." Therefore we can understand the admonitions from Jesus and the apostles to concentrate our thoughts and efforts on the good things—those positive energies that act as seeds to produce more good fruit of peace, joy, and love.

In reading through the book *The Master Key System* by Charles F. Haanel some years ago, the concept of gratitude grabbed my interest. The book was originally published in 1912 and teaches the concepts of positive mental attitude. In a nutshell, he taught that by practicing true gratitude on a consistent basis and actually feeling the emotions of such, the energy focus of a person could be shifted to a more pleasant and productive positive attitude and lifestyle of gratitude. As I read on, I found the concept to be in agreement and consistent with scriptural principles of faith I had read for years. Oddly though, I had to confess that I had put far too much attention and spent too much of my energy on negative issues, and as a result my gratitude factor, although somewhat active, was found to be lacking. Consequently by not regularly expressing and feeling sincere gratitude and only praying "thank you" prayers from a minor standpoint, I was experiencing more negative things in my life than I should have been. It was as if my "life scale" was found to have been somewhat weighted on the negative side and I didn't realize it as such. After some serious soul searching and being brutally honest with myself, I found that many more things were present for me to be grateful for than things

> I found that many more things were present for me to be grateful for than things to be unhappy about.

to be unhappy about. I prayed and asked for help to get this issue straightened out and the results have been nothing short of miraculous. All during my days and nights, I find myself stating to the Lord the many things I am grateful for. By doing so, I have found that more good things come to light each time I pray and along with being thankful for eternal life, true peace, great health, an enjoyable occupation, a wonderful and blessed wife, healthy children, opportunities to share the good news, and many other things, additional blessings seem to come to the forefront for me to be grateful for.

Living a life of gratitude really does produce more areas in life to be grateful for, and dwelling on the blessings takes our personal energy away from the negativity that craves our attention. Although negative issues do arise, they possess far less power than before and seem to pass by at a distance rather than spending time up close. When I first began to fervently practice the gratitude idea, a small rock in my pocket was a reminder to think of all that I should be grateful and thankful for. I no longer need that little rock as a token because I have grown to live my life in gratitude. Every morning as I open my eyes and all during the day I am thankful to God for my blessings. Throughout the day when I am not in conversation with someone else, I am usually in a "gratitude session" with the Lord who blesses with more than I can realize and far more than I can know. The Worry Monster no longer leaves unwanted deposits on my living room rug because he's been flushed from the house! True peace comes naturally with abiding gratitude and is a subject often discussed but generally unfamiliar to the multitudes.

Negative energy cannot prevail where gratitude abides.

> Negative energy cannot prevail where gratitude abides.

Experiencing the indwelling of gratitude has introduced me to a form of peace I sought for decades and thankfully now know as a daily regimen—a form of provisional daily bread.

When praying the Lord's Prayer, comprehension of all we have to be thankful for in every verse should be a natural product of the all-encompassing nature of the prayer. I am grateful for the perfection, fullness, and positive energy in the prayer taught by Jesus and for His place as the Holy Spirit that dwells within me.

Peace Brother!

In the introductions and greetings found in many of the New Testament books, the word "peace" is found as an indication of its importance in the life of the believer. Peace in this sense and in numerous other verses is defined as "set at one again, quietness, rest" and is generally used in the same context today. I have also used the word numerous times throughout this book as it is such a great part of my life, and I feel more should be noted by expanding on the idea of indwelling peace touched on in the last chapter. Peace cannot be purchased but can be possessed freely by understanding the atmosphere that attracts it into the heart. It is listed as a "fruit" of the spirit in Galatians 5:22, third in the line-up after love and joy.

The Old Testament prophet Isaiah, during what is believed to be the eighth century BC, wrote a prophecy of a coming birth of one who would be called the "Prince of Peace":

"For unto us a Child is born, unto us a Son is given; and the government shall be upon His shoulder. And His name will be called Wonderful, Counselor, Mighty God, Everlasting Father, **Prince of Peace**. Of the increase of His government and peace there will be no end."

Though portions of the prophecy are yet to be fulfilled, it is quite obvious that the "Child" spoken of is Jesus.

And hundreds of years later, just as prophecy of His birth dictated, the Child was born. The words of Jesus during His ministry can be found in John 14:27 as He issues a special gift and grant of His peace.

"Peace I leave with you, My peace I give to you; not as the world gives do I give to you. Let not your heart be troubled, neither let it be afraid."

> Though not widely recognized as such, fear is specifically addressed by scripture as a "spirit," and according to scripture, is not given by God.

We are told by this verse that the peace granted by Jesus is different from the world's view of peace and hearts should not be troubled, worried, or agitated (according to the definition of the word in Strong's *Exhaustive Concordance of the Bible)*. The verse also addresses fear and the admonition not to let it have presence in the heart. The point in discussing fear is that peace cannot have presence when fear is allowed to rule. Fear is negative energy and usually is destructive in many forms by its nature, while peace is completely positive, constructive, and uplifting energy. The whole discussion of fear and peace boils down to a central point, which is we can choose to live in fear and have no peace or live in peace without the oppression of fear. One or the other; but the energies cannot co-exist. Though not widely recognized as such, fear is specifically addressed by scripture as a "spirit," and according to scripture, is not given by God. So if God does not give fear, guess who does. A careful reading of 2 Timothy 1:7 should shed some light:

"For God has not given us a **spirit** of fear, but of power, and of love and of a sound mind."

We are warned by the Bible to test the spirits whether they are of God, or not. In this verse, it is plainly stated that fear is NOT given by God and is classified as a spirit. As such, it is sent to prevent peace and squelch faith. So, once again it becomes easy to see that when fear is allowed to exist, faith and peace are absent.

Peace, on the other hand, is a wonderful gift of God. However, much like presents under the Christmas tree, the gift will never be enjoyed until it is accepted, unwrapped, and used as it should be. The peace we have been given can only be experienced if fully accepted and invited into our heart by our faith in its reality, and by believing in and acting upon the power of its presence.

The presence of peace can occasionally be intruded upon by the spirit of fear, but only when it is allowed to exercise some control. Without faith peace cannot be found, but the powers of peace and faith, if practiced, easily overcome any visitation by fear and its sidekicks, known as worry and doubt. By knowing that the spirit of fear is not sent by God, it can be over powered and sent away by the truth found in the scripture previously quoted from 2nd Timothy 1:7. So the expected question would be—how does a person confront a spirit?

When Jesus was tempted by Satan in the desert, He defeated Satan by the power of the word of God, and we have been granted power to do the same. Knowing that

God has **not** given the Spirit of fear is one thing. But being confident of what he has provided, namely power, love, and a **sound** mind, is imperative to maintain true and lasting peace in our lives. Even though it may feel strange at the onset, verbally addressing the spirit of fear and proclaiming from the scripture that God has provided power, love, and a sound mind will take the bite out of the battle and provide a much firmer foothold to stand in faith and confess peace. It is a great idea to memorize the scripture and quote it often as a reminder of one of the great gifts granted to all believers.

During the previously stated lengthy and painful period of my life, even as a Christian the abiding presence of real peace seemed illusive at best. I know all about the problems of living without it and was well versed in acting as if everything was alright even when it wasn't. After discovering the key to free myself and finding the formula for true peace, I no longer live in oppression or denial as before. The choice is mine in refusing to live with doubt in my life and by that refusal I openly accept the blessing of peace. We are all created and blessed with a free will to accept or reject what we want or don't want and I simply accepted the blessing of peace. I pray in peace, think and speak in terms of peace, and live the life I have been given with it as my banner. When my harmony is occasionally attacked or when I mess things up, the situation is recognized for what it is and swiftly

> The path is called "faith" and the ditches on each side are fear and doubt.

corrected in order to return to the blessings of tranquility. Above all things, I seek to live in peace with God and my fellow man. Believe it or not, it is readily available for all who seek it by simply letting go of the steering wheel, once gripped in fear, and allowing our Lord to get us safely to our destination by the path and direction of His choice. The path is called "faith" and the ditches on each side are fear and doubt. A peaceful countenance produces more seeds of the same and opens a heightened understanding of having love and trust actively working in our lives. Jesus expressed ultimate trust and love for the Father by praying "nevertheless, not what I will, but what you will," as recorded in Mark 14:36.

Stillness, in an obedient spiritual form, can only be experienced when peace is present. When in prayerful stillness, or meditation in the peaceful presence of God, the comforting voice of His guidance and love can be experienced. The presence of God does truly exist, and His love for humanity is known in the lives of multitudes.

So many voices today cry out, "How do I find God?" God's word answers "Be still and know that I am God."

A Word About Words

When talking to groups of people about personal communication and the power and energy carried by the words we use, I find that many are surprised to discover the potency accompanying the words we all use every day. During many of the talks I give a working example by conducting a group experiment during the meeting that usually goes something like this:

"Everyone please close your eyes and mentally put away anything that would distract your attention just for the next few minutes. I ask you to take a mental trip with me to the beach. You have left the hotel room and are walking on the warm concrete of the hotel pool deck. As you step onto the wood boardwalk leading to the sand you can feel the uneven areas of the boards, and walking through the sugary sand, the tiny granules work their way between your toes. As you sit on the beach chair and relax, the warm sun and beach breeze feel calming and welcoming on your skin. The sound of the surf is peaceful and tranquil. You smell the familiar salt air. Physical relaxation begins to release any tensions you previously had and all you feel right now is gratitude and peace for this place, this feeling, and this beach. Does everyone have the place firmly fixed in your mind? Can you feel it? Good!

Now we are going to leave the beach (usually at this transition I hear multiple sighs of protest) and we're going to a place in the country. Through a sunlit field of small yellow flowers, we see a slight hill with a huge, beautiful tree at the very top and a shaded area of lush green grass below it. The little flowers in the field sway in the breeze and the temperature beneath the tree is perfect. Do you have this place firmly fixed in your mind? Great!

> Words are important tools and should be used with great discretion and wisdom because of the power they possess and their potential to create lasting effects."

Now without any further direction from me, slowly return to your place on the beach and experience it as before with all the sights, senses, and emotions."

I usually give the group a few minutes to enjoy the beach once again and then call their attention back to the meeting.

After they have stretched and their eyes have adjusted to the light, I reveal my point for the exercise. With the power of only my words, each of you has allowed me to enter your mind and paint pictures of places that evoke your senses and your emotions, resulting in the sensation of physical relaxation. Those places and feelings are there to stay and will be there anytime you wish to return to either the beach or to the peaceful knoll beneath the tree. Those wonderful places came into being today in your mind because of my suggestion and your reception of the words, but you felt the feelings and saw the sights that brought you peace and pleasure and you probably now feel physically and mentally relaxed because of the experience. That is the power of words at work and the point of this demonstration.

If we delve into what makes words from a purely physical standpoint, they are the simple result of vibrations of the air from our lungs passing through the vocal cords and controlled by the tongue and lips to produce differing resonance levels. When the articulated resonances are linked together along with input from our emotions, sounds are formed corresponding to ideas and images already programmed into the brain.

But the words we use have another aspect which is far more compelling. The words are accompanied by forms of energy that affect our senses, our emotions, and even the way we think of someone else or ourselves. The energy carried in the emotion with which the word is delivered has a direct effect on personal energies of the person speaking and the person hearing the communication. Basically, words can evoke positive or negative energy in the person producing or receiving the communication. Need proof? Let's just use one simple word. The word is "Hello."

Now, out loud say "Hello" as if you are seeing a dear loved one you haven't seen for a long time. Say it with the emotions of love and satisfaction you would feel at the sight of their smiling face. That "Hello" sounds wonderful and oozes positive energy and love. Now, imagine that it is Monday morning with everything going on at one time and peace is nowhere to be found in the office. Among the multitudes of phone calls all needing your attention or attempting to sell you something, someone calls you by dialing the wrong number. After they have called and interrupted your important work twice, you see the same number the third time on the caller I.D. screen. After imagining this scenario in detail, say "Hello" in the manner you can imagine, considering the third aggravating imposition by this multiple offender.

What energy did this latter "Hello" carry and what message was conveyed by the same single word? Quite a different contrast from the "Hello" for a returning loved one. So there we have it—the same word producing completely different emotionally-charged energies and intents. The first greeting filled with positive energy of love and the second one all negative. Now imagine receiving a phone call saying that something terrible had happened to one of your children. The first thing you would experience is a sickening feeling in the pit of your stomach, of course followed by fear and serious emotional outpouring. But the point here is the words you received actually affected not only your emotions but your physical body and your internal organs as well, maybe even to the point of physical sickness. All of these emotions and feelings have been the result of the energy "vibrations" carried by the words used and the emotion that propelled them into becoming part of your life experience.

According to the laws of physics, energy cannot be created or destroyed, but it can be transformed or changed. Scientific studies and electronic devices have shown that all things, including humans, have energy fields within and without that can be mapped electronically, such as seen with MRI testing. The human outer energy field is sometimes referred to as an aura and will change configuration and coloration with differing sensory and energetic forms of input. Our energy fields can be affected by any number of outside influences, depending on verbal, mental, and physical receptions. Words in particular, with their corresponding influences and mode of delivery, have the ability and power to result in any number of changes at all levels. We all act as powerful transmitters and receivers, and as such possess potentials of energy manipulation beyond what is commonly realized.

The spoken or written word contains the ability to make us laugh or cause tears of sorrow. Words actually have the capacity to reach into the depths of the human heart and create any range of emotions from love to shame and compassion to disdain. With the proper use of words, we have the ability to paint a color picture upon the inner workings of the human brain that will remain there indefinitely. To the recipient, a negatively charged misspoken string of words may be forgiven, but the message conveyed will never be forgotten because the spoken word cannot be erased. Our use of verbal or written communication can be our best asset or our worst enemy. Our words can bring about the joy of enlightenment or the darkened confusion of misunderstanding, and the choice to create any of these scenarios is within our capabilities and will to do so.

> Our use of verbal or written communication can be our best asset or our worst enemy.

From another angle, the book of John chapter 1, verse 1 says, "In the beginning was the Word, and the Word was with

God, and the Word was God." Notice the capitalization of "Word." Verse 3 goes on to state, "All things were made through Him, and without Him nothing was made that was made." Strong's *Exhaustive Concordance of the Bible* defines "Word" in this context as "something said, also reasoning or motive," which is essentially the same general definition with which we are accustomed. The extremely interesting message in this scripture is that the creative aspect of God is called "Word." Everything was and apparently still is made or created by the Word, attesting again to the power of the Word (defined as "something said"). A study could be made from this avenue that could end up in another book, but the point has been made duly attesting to the creativity of a word or Word, such as the case may be. In short, words equate to creativity in many differing forms.

My motivation for this discussion is to point out the arrangement and use of not only the choice of words and their placement in the Lord's Prayer but also that the emotions and intentions accompanying and propelling the spoken words in the prayer and any other spiritual communication should be considered above everything else. Conversely, mindless repetition of a string of insincere memorized verbiage is a vain waste of valuable time from both physical

> James 1:26 states, "If anyone among you thinks he is religious, and does not bridle his tongue but deceives his own heart, this one's religion is useless."

and spiritual aspects. Is it possible that calling upon our Lord to listen to this type of prayer could be considered "taking the Lord's name in vain" or irreverently calling upon Him for no constructive purpose? While we all know that God's last name is not "dammit," there are far bigger fish to fry when considering various aspects of "taking His name in vain."

We have been endowed with the ability to express our emotions in various ways, but words are by far our most commonly used and most commonly misused form of expression. Proper use of this precious blessing, from a biblical standpoint, is considered an important issue. James 1:26 states, "If anyone among you thinks he is religious, and does not bridle his tongue but deceives his own heart, this one's religion is useless." The gravity of this scripture is further verified in James 3:2, "For we all stumble in many things. If anyone does not stumble in word, he is a perfect (mature) man, able also to bridle the whole body." Jesus is quoted in Matthew 15:17-18, "Do you not yet understand that whatever enters the mouth goes into the stomach and is eliminated? But those things which proceed out of the mouth come from the heart, and they defile the man." There are many more scriptures that speak of the importance of the use of our words, but for the sake of brevity, the verses listed here should be enough to make the point that what we speak is an indicator of what lives in our hearts.

The life, death, and resurrection of Jesus changed not only the world but eternal destinies as well, but it was His words that were and still are used to describe His story. As previously noted in this book, John's gospel 1:1 declared "the Word was God" only to expand on the theme in verse 14 to explain, "And the Word became flesh and dwelt among us, and we beheld His glory, the glory as the only begotten of the Father." The "only begotten of the Father," also referred to as the Word, spoke into creation words of comfort and peace that produced healing and forgiveness of sins for all mankind. Even now, some 2000 years later, His words still speak life, love, joy, and remain alive to bless us forever.

> What will the echo of the words we've spoken testify about us when we're gone from the earth?

What will the echo of the words we've spoken testify about us when we're gone from the earth? It will be those words that memorialize the essence of our lives in the hearts of those who remember our time here. Very few people remember the inscription on a tomb stone, but it could be that some of our words will live on for years or decades to come in the memories of those we knew. How will those remembrances sound and what emotions and energies will they invoke? Will our heavenly Father be pleased with the words we've left for others?

Don't Push the Rope

During our individualized journeys in this earthly incarnation, spiritually oriented people seem to figure out that our true purposes for being here should be explored and acted upon. From a personal viewpoint, I am not a believer in coincidence or happenstance, or that lives and the situations surrounding them are a random shotgun blast into the segment of time we are chosen to encounter. There are reasons for all of us to be here, in this time, in the locations and areas of influence we occupy. The complete or even partial discovery of the reason for our existence unfortunately seems to be seriously pondered by a relatively small number of people today who take the time from their busy lives to contemplate such things. Life and the turbulent stage play that surrounds it has a way of spawning innumerable distractions that, if allowed, can weave their way into every fiber of our being and choke the connections of spiritual communication. Ironically, the bulk of those distractions, so high on some personal lists, are usually found to have little or no meaningful, spiritual, or lasting substance. They just take up lots of time and personal energy as the endless beat goes on and on and the dance of the holographic distraction continues. Finding one's life purpose or dharma, as it is referred to in eastern philosophies, should be the central quest and general goal of our time in this life. In the search to excavate the treasure of the personal dharma, many truths concerning God's highest and best plan for our life journey can be uncovered. In believing we are created by the Most High God, we have to believe we are created for specific purposes. As the Bible states, we are here for the purpose of glorifying God, and simply being a "what-not" on the cosmic curio shelf with no other reason than to collect dust is probably not in the over-all plan.

> What is it that you really want in this life"?

Some years ago during a weekend silent retreat I attended, a Jesuit priest in closing the first talk of a series asked, "aside from all the tangible things we see, hear, touch, smell, and so on, what is it that you really want in this life"? The emphasis of the question was placed on the word "really." He noted that some of the guys may find the answer in a relatively short time while others may take weeks, months, and possibly years to find an answer. But some, he said, may sadly never find the answer to this most important riddle of life. While mentally and prayerfully sorting through the possibilities for what we wanted above everything else, we would most likely all come closer to finding the key to unlock the doors of our individual life purposes and missions. The priest finished his talk that afternoon by noting our answer to his question, if discovered, was to remain purely personal and kept strictly between us and God.

That question, along with the depth of soul searching it requires, is frequently revisited and meditated upon during my devotional times even now as a spiritual check up of sorts. I have known for decades that my life had a reason for being and that many people probably had the same thoughts concerning purpose and intent. But in years past, to put the proverbial finger on a specific point was only guessed at and speculated upon.

Tonight, as I took a break from writing and set out on the nightly walk with our little dog, Susie, under the clear night sky, I felt gratitude for the generally moderate fall and winter weather we enjoy here in south Louisiana. We walked on in the night breeze and I prayed as I always do while Susie enjoyed the highlight of her day—sniffing everything within nose range. That question posed years ago revisited my mind and I thanked God for the blessing of knowing as I have known for many years what I really desired during this present earthly incarnation. Confusion no longer holds a place in my life and fear of the unknown has long since been replaced by faith in the truth of what I know. One of the things I know is that prayers of gratitude always expand into additional positive, constructive prayers along with blessings of faith and hope. In the fourth and final chapter of Philippians, beginning in the eighth verse, the Apostle Paul records, "Finally brethren, whatever things are true, whatever things are noble, whatever things are just, whatever things are pure, whatever things are lovely, whatever things are of good report, if there is anything praiseworthy—meditate on these things."

Paul was obviously a man who had attained great wisdom and learned to live a life of gratitude in remembrance of all the things by which we are continually blessed. He had certainly suffered greatly for his preaching, considered controversial and revolutionary during that time. But his understanding of the importance of this brief life when compared to the endlessness of eternity was evident in his writings of Romans 8:18, "For I consider that the sufferings of this present time are not worthy to be compared with the glory which shall be revealed in us." Later in the 28th verse of the same chapter he added, "And we know that all things work together for good to those who love God and are called according to His purpose." It is in the personal call to a spiritual purpose that we will find the answer to the priest's question because the answer lies within the doing of God's spiritual will while still in our physical body. Hence, the co-existence and marriage of the spiritual and the physical in demonstration of the fulfilling of God's will during earthly existence. The divine importance of our earthly visitation, although brief, cannot be overstated.

Many spend their entire adulthood paddling madly downstream to get ahead of the other boats in the river in order to "win" the all important social and financial race they believe exists. Their lives consist of an endless striving to achieve an elusive goal perceived as worldly success and status. Like the mad paddler, when they get closer to a gathering point in the river, reality comes into focus as multitudes of people and boats already waiting beyond the imagined finish line enjoy and recall the lessons learned while quietly floating on the river. It is at this point the exhausted paddler becomes cognizant of his misconception and discovers that he was never in a race in the first place, but merely sharing the same river with others who were enjoying blessings and surroundings of their peaceful outing. At the gathering, he hears the conversations of the others recounting the beautiful scenery along the river banks while being propelled by the river current. But he has no recollection of the banks or the scenery. He was far too busy and focused in his quest to pass the other boats to notice that they did not use or need paddles. He never heard their voices and the invitations to join them over the noise of his own motivation and his self-centered concentration. The continual moderate but powerful flow of the river carried the others along without effort, affording them the enjoyment of the river itself and the natural beauty revealed along the banks. At the festive get-together the paddler had nothing to share or offer the others because his focus was on the self-imposed race and upon his own push to win what could not be won. To his dismay, there was no competition. He was now forced to do something diametrically opposed to his polished ego and now only listen and for once not control every conversation and manipulate every outcome. In the end, the paddler would hear of some of the lessons learned and attempt to imagine the joy and wisdom that blessed the others, but only from their recollections, not his own. The river of life flows for all who seek the tranquil waters put in motion to carry us along the path of a peaceful and beneficial existence. Any attempt to hurry or change the river's current is futile and no ego can force a change in its purpose or direction. The river's energy, created and directed by God, has been there forever and will always continue its flow toward the eternal kingdom. Its peaceful nature is constant and unchanging. It seeks not to control but to assist life journeys, but the assistance is granted only in direct proportion to our submission to the river's direction and power.

My personal answer to the priest's question was and is that above everything else, I seek for the deep and lasting peace of God's will to prevail in my life and that I might share it with as many people as possible. This book is a part of that philosophy. God's purpose for my purpose came into focus because I chose to allow the current in the river to carry me along as I learned to be still and hear the peaceful voice of the river itself.

I walked on through our neighborhood with Susie, enjoying the evening with peace, gratitude, and praise framing my prayers. I thanked God for His continual presence and the calm assurance of knowing that above all things my relationship with Him is the most important point of this present life and the continuance of my life after transcending the earthly dimension. His constant indwelling and the peace of that understanding alone brings a welcome end to the "search for God" that is heard of so often these days. I don't have to beg and plead for God to be with me; He's here. I don't have to travel the world in search of Him and His presence or for relics to prove His existence. When Diane and I look deeply into each other's eyes, His

> I don't have to beg and plead for God to be with me; He's here. I don't have to travel the world in search of Him and His presence or for relics to prove His existence.

presence is there, without a doubt. An old saying we've all heard is, "the eyes are the mirror of our soul" and it is true because I have seen it. The Bible says that God's spirit will never leave us or forsake us, and I believe that just as it is written. That precious temple within has doors that never close and windows filled with light, and a book containing my name among countless others. Knowing that He knows my needs even better than I do is a huge relief and takes away the deception that I need to dictate what should be done in my life by directing which of His blessings should be bestowed upon me at any given time. Would I rather live this life attempting to push the rope of my own ego-centered ideas, or is it more feasible to be led by the golden cord of infinite intelligence? After all, it is by His will that I take another breath, or not. It is by His bidding that people are put in my path to help me or to be helped by me or to just enjoy the fellowship. It was by His direction that the relationship with my wife began so that we together would embark on this life journey of ever unfolding spiritual discovery during our time together. It is by His grace that when this life on earth comes to an end, we will live on in eternity as a part of God. The truth is that we are all one heartbeat away from that transcendence to a

> The truth is that we are all one heartbeat away from that transcendence to a completely spiritual consciousness and our Father holds the key to it all.

completely spiritual consciousness and our Father holds the key to it all. Along with the peace of knowing all this we have the assurance that things in this life work together for ultimate good for those who love Him and are called according to His purpose. In this earthly body, the all-encompassing presence we call God has given us a spiritual heart that acts as a filter from which we can know the difference between truth and deception, but only if we quiet our own voice in order to hear its beckoning.

God calls out to us to "Be still" in order to experience and enjoy that quiet and peaceful place where our spirits unify in the corporate body and presence of the Almighty. This coming together of kindred spirits serves to fine tune our awareness to the truth that our individual spirits were never separated from each other in the first place as we are all part of the body. Genesis 1:26 reminds us that we are all created equally in the image and likeness of God who has been, is, and will forever be Our Father who is in heaven.

Parting Words

This book has been written and is delivered to the readers with the sincere hope that the prayer we call "The Lord's Prayer" will be better understood and more effectively prayed with a firmer and wider foundation. Interpretations of passages should be treated as opinions of the author and should never be considered as all inclusive. God in His wisdom supplies answers to our individual inquiries with His enlightening at His choosing and the time and place that is most beneficial to us. When praying, the "stillness" aspect may be employed between passages that a deeper connection with Our Lord may be experienced and that His voice may be heard within the prevailing peace.

It is the hope and prayer of the author that ideas revealed in the personal revelations written here will be expanded upon through spiritual understanding given freely to all who seek God's wisdom, will, and abiding presence. May our prayers be frequent and fervent. May the words we present before God be ever loving, well chosen, and reverent. And may the light of the Holy Spirit within us continually increase, illuminating every area of our lives, our souls, and our spirits so that we may comprehend the blessing of unity with God.

The End

BOUNDLESS VISION

To see with boundless vision
Through eyes that never close
Across the sea of crystal faith
Where love forever flows…

To share the dream with those who have not
To conceive what can surely be
To sow life and love in a previous void
To dream – To believe – To be

By Michael T. Abadie
April 22, 1997

About the Author

Michael T. Abadie is a "Chaplain at Large" for motorcyclists and is the author of Shiny Side Up. As a freelance writer, he is a regular contributor for various magazines and has been featured as a guest speaker on radio talk shows and at social gatherings. Michael T. and his wife Diane reside in Baton Rouge, Louisiana, with their dog, Susie.